TB

BILTON

BASICS

FOREWORD
by Brian Turner CBE

It's always good to feel an affinity with someone and I suppose that being a fellow Yorkshireman does help. Well it does, doesn't it?

Timothy Bilton is a man after my own heart. I share his belief in Yorkshire's produce being the finest and I enthusiastically support his dedication in training young people both professionally at college and through the junior chef's academy on a Saturday morning.

Not only that but this lad can cook a bit, as his track record shows. So many awards are testament to his decision to work with only the top people and at the top places.

Yorkshire is now privileged to have Tim at the helm of The Butchers Arms which goes from strength to strength. All Tim and I need now is for Leeds United to get back to where they truly belong and we will be two very happy Yorkshiremen.

This book is about what is good in our home county and is written for all to enjoy and learn, so please enjoy and learn from Tim.

Brian Turner CBE

ACKNOWLEDGEMENTS

Where to start? Firstly I'd like to thank **David and Maxine**, otherwise known as mother and father-in-law, mum and dad, grandma and grandad, babysitter, odd-job man, photographer, project manager and the man who fixes everything when it goes wrong. But without David the book and our business could not function. I look forward to the future with great anticipation, with your support nothing can go wrong ... Can it?

To **our customers** past, present and future.

I would like to thank my core team of staff (**Team TB!**) for your dedication and hard work towards every aspect of my business and for having the vision and goal as myself.

A very big thank you to **Lucy Duncan** for generally doing everything and anything for me the minute I ask for it (I am not a patient man!) and for putting up with my various moods and for being my punch bag when I am at the top of my tree! Thank you Lucy.

To **Alan Jones**, my first real employer at The Swiss Cottage, Wentbridge. You instilled into me so much that I have carried with me for my entire working career.

To **Martyn Lipp** my old college lecturer at Wakefield College when I first started out in the chef world. Now, after all these years, we find ourselves back working together. I have all the prep that I could want. As they say in the trade, "Happiness is a mise-en-place tray".

To everyone I have had the pleasure, or otherwise, of working with. You have all touched my working career in one way or another.

To **Raymond Blanc**, the Master, thank you.

To my dedicated and passionate suppliers. Without your endeavours to deliver the very best I would not be able to produce what I do… **Jeremy and Louise at Yummy Yorkshire**, **Carl at Greedy Little Pig**, **Jenny and Richard (Dick) at Round Green Farm, Brindon at Brindon Addys Butchers, Steve at Doric Game, James at Wellocks, Justin at Staal smokehouse, Chris at Sailbrand, Alison Dodds at Herbs Unlimited, Garry at Hallgarten wine.**

Martin Edwards and **Paul Cocker** at **RMC Books** thank you for your belief and vision. I look forward to the next chapter. **Susan Pape** thank you for sorting my recipes, coping with my bad spellings, grammar and typing my illegible sentences.

To my **mum** you still give me the drive today that you did when I was young. I will see you again one day.

And lastly but never ever least to my wife **Adele** and two boys **Henry and Charlie** without you none of this would be worth doing.

It's all for you x x x. You are my world. TB.

CONTENTS

TIMOTHY BILTON

Where it all began...

This is not a self-aware chef's book. It's a cookery book that I hope will put some of the skill back into cooking. There are no foams or water baths – just good basic cookery. We'll be looking at areas such as poaching, baking, roasting, steaming, frying …

Master these and you can cook anything.

I want you to be able to thumb through this book and see how to cook – in a simple and straightforward way.

I became interested in cookery as a small boy living in Ferrybridge, in my native Yorkshire, when I watched my grandma produce the most amazing Sunday lunches for my whole family – including aunts and uncles – and I could never understand how she did that from an ordinary domestic oven.

I first discovered professional cooking at a restaurant called the Swiss Cottage at Wentbridge, near Pontefract. I was 13 and needed extra pocket money and got a job washing up. The kitchen was massive and there was a real buzz about the place with eight chefs working in the hot, steamy atmosphere – it was electric. From that moment, I was hooked.

I became enchanted with the likes of the Roux brothers, Marco Pierre White and Raymond Blanc and wanted to be like them so, after leaving school, I went to college to do a European Chef's Diploma. One of my lecturers was Martyn Lipp – who now works with me at The Butchers Arms as prep chef.

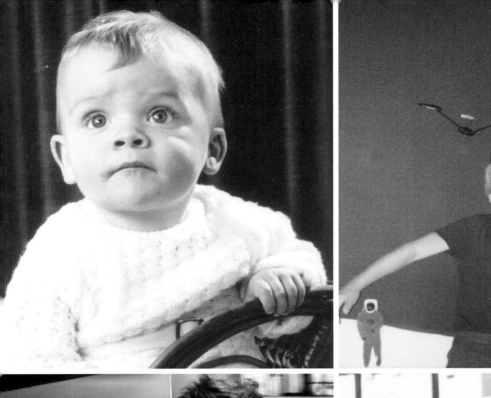

Le Manoir aux Quat'Saisons

Martyn organised a work placement for me at Le Manoir aux Quat'Saisons and it worked out so well that I ended up working there for two years when I finished my Diploma course. I worked in every part of the kitchen. It was hard work and long hours but I learned so much – it was a fantastic experience for a young chef and I'll always be grateful to Monsieur Raymond for all he taught me.

After Le Manoir I moved to the south of France to fulfil a romantic notion that I had about French cuisine, and worked with Yves Thuriès at the Hostellerie du Vieux Cordes in the Tarn region.

When I came back to Yorkshire, I had the idea that I should teach the next generation of chefs and completed a teaching qualification at Huddersfield University before going to teach for six years at what was then the Thomas Danby College in Leeds.

After meeting my wife, Adele, and having the first of our two boys, Henry (our second son is called Charlie), we needed extra income so I took a part time job at Bibis in Leeds. I became absolutely enthralled with the vastness of the kitchen, the camaraderie of the chefs and the vibrancy of the restaurant – and ended up taking a full-time job there.

But I had always wanted my own place and one wet, cold February day I quite literally stumbled across a pub, which was clearly failing and, believe me, was absolutely grotty. When I walked through the door I had an epiphany – I envisaged how it could be and that's how it is now: The Butchers Arms is exactly as I imagined it that day.

We are not everything to everyone because I think restaurants can spread themselves too thinly. We're a high-end gastro pub offering modern British cuisine with a twist – and good quality food that is largely locally produced.

The other thing I insist on is using food that is in season. I'm a chef who looks forward to the different seasons – starting in January with forced rhubarb; spring for asparagus; the summer months for nice soft berries and delicate herbs; autumn for pumpkins, squashes and the start of the game season; and December when it's freezing cold for turkeys, sprouts and parsnips.

And we must be doing something right because we've got a string of awards to our name including Pub Restaurant Chef Award from the Craft Guild of Chefs; Best Gastro Pub from the Great British Pub Awards; Best use of Regional Produce on the Menu from the Deliciouslyorkshire Awards; Yorkshire Life's Dining Pub Award; and The Publican's Food Pub and Best Newcomer awards.

I've also appeared on BBC Two's Great British Menu, twice.

It all seems a long way from grandma's back doorstep – but it's been a fascinating journey – and now I want to share some of it with you.

METHODS
of Cookery

I once saw a recipe in a cookbook which began "sweat the mirepoix*…"

While that means something to professional chefs like me, I daresay it'd be gobbledegook to most people. To my mind, a cookbook which leaves you baffled after three words isn't much use.

So let's begin at the beginning. As Mrs Beeton might say, first take your food.

Now match it to the best cooking method. Consider the flavours, textures and appearance of the finished dish, and judge the length of time required for cooking it to perfection.

Bob's your uncle. You can now cook. But just before you rush off to receive your Michelin star, take a moment to look at our simple guide to getting the best from the various methods at your disposal.

Let's start by dividing our methods into either moist or dry. Into the former category are boiling, poaching, braising or stewing, whereas dry would be classed as roasting and baking. It is not uncommon for both to be required for a particular dish.

Recipes are the guide for the chef or cook, most of them founded on traditional techniques and processes. Once you understand them, you're in a position to experiment. But do so carefully. Whereas you can sometimes adjust a recipe for some food, other dishes are more of a science.

* For those who were wondering, a mirepoix consists of five basic vegetables which are used to establish a lot of sauces and gravies. The ones I use are chopped onion, celery, a leek, a carrot and garlic. To sweat is simply to cook without colour – just enough to release the flavour.

BOILING

Simple this. Cooking in liquid at 100°C.

It's one of the most widely used cookery methods and is used in the preparation of stocks, sauces, soups, pasta, rice, shellfish, vegetables, poultry and meat.

Where boiling for a long period of time is required (e.g. ham hocks), the liquid will need to be topped up from time to time to ensure that the meat is totally covered and evenly cooked. Use a lid to aid the boiling process in this case but the same doesn't apply to vegetables, which must be kept uncovered, likewise pasta and rice, which needs to be stirred occasionally to prevent sticking.

Be sure to cook vegetables, pasta and rice in plenty of boiling salted water. Don't be tempted to cook too much at once as this can cause an uneven result. Check your vegetables etc can move freely in the pan.

For most meat and poultry it is essential to skim the liquid when it first comes to the boil. This prevents the deposits boiling back into the liquid and spoiling the finishing sauce. Gentle boiling helps break down the fibrous structure of meat such as ham hocks, which would be tough if cooked by another method.

Deep boiling is what the name suggests. Starting cooking in cold water or stock before bringing to the boil, this helps to extract the flavour of meats.

Conversely, add food such as green vegetables straight to boiling water, this creates a far more vibrant and appealing colour. Just be sure the pan has reached boiling point as if not the vegetables will discolour.

POACHING

Many foods call for poaching, be it in milk or stock. The big difference from boiling is that the optimum temperature of the liquid is lower, around 93-95°C. It's commonly used to cook everything from fish fillets to fruits.

There are two main types of poaching:

Deep poaching – where the item is totally submerged in liquid but unlike boiling there is no movement of the liquid. Stock or other liquid will impart flavour to the item being poached.

Shallow poaching – this involves placing food such as fish, poultry or game into a buttered dish with the minimum amount of liquid, a buttered paper lid to prevent the food from drying out and cooking in the oven at approximately 180°C. Ideally, bring the liquid to the boil before placing in the oven.

STEWING

Typically, a combination of meat and vegetables, slow-cooked in the oven to give a rich result.

If made correctly, there should be enough sauce in the stew to serve at the correct consistency without adding a thickening agent. But care should be taken not to overcook as this can cause evaporation of the liquid and a breakdown of the component foods.

COOKING IN GOOSE FAT (CONFIT)

This is a great way of cooking meat and poultry, which becomes moist and flavoursome.

In a tray or container scatter Cornish sea salt, black pepper and some twigs of thyme. Place the meat or poultry on top and repeat with the salt, pepper and thyme. Cover and place in the fridge for 24 hours. This will help get rid of any excess water from the meat. Take the meat out of the fridge, discard any water in the bottom of the tray, and rub with kitchen towel to remove excess salt, pepper and thyme and dry the meat.

Place into a deep-sided tray and cover with goose fat. Cover the tray with greaseproof paper and then cook in a moderate oven at approximately 150ºC. When cooked, the flesh should give easily but not fall apart. Remove from the fat and allow cooling time.

The goose fat can be passed through a sieve, refrigerated and used again.

Before serving, briefly heat in the oven to crisp the skin.

Examples of cooking times in goose fat:
Duck legs: 2 hours 15 minutes
Rabbit legs: 2 hours
Pork belly: 2 hours 30 minutes
Pork shin: 1 hour 30 minutes
Pheasant legs: 1 hour 15 minutes

BRAISING

Braising is my personal favourite method. I suppose that it's a mixture of stewing and pot roasting.

It's most suited to tougher joints of meat and poultry which require a longer cooking time. Vegetables such as leeks, fennel, chicory and cabbage can also be braised.

Crucially, with meat the process normally starts with shallow frying to seal, colour and flavour the outer surface. Combine this with base vegetables – for example onion, carrots, leeks, celery and garlic – and then liquid such as stock or wine. Tomatoes and herbs can be added to give the sauce flavour.

ROASTING

There can be few greater joys in life than a perfect roast potato. This cooking method can turn the humble spud into a delicious adventure in texture and flavour.

But roasting also delivers great results with prime quality tender joints of meat, poultry and game.

It's essential there is an adequate covering of fat to melt through the meat and keep the roast moist. If there is no fat then larding is required (inserting strips of fat into the meat or covering it with fat to prevent the meat from drying out in the roasting process).

Larding is vital with most game birds as well as some poultry.

Vegetables such as potatoes, parsnips, carrots, celeriac and sweet potatoes are a classic autumn/winter dish roasted together on the same tray. Roasting produces characteristic flavours, because the surface protein of the food is sealed in, preventing the escape of too many natural juices.

Tips and techniques with roasting:
Always pre-heat the oven.
Cooking time varies according to whether meat is on or off the bone.
Always allow the meat to rest for at least 15 minutes after roasting before carving.

A couple of commonly-used roasting terms:
Trussing – the tying of poultry with string to help keep its shape.
Basting – spooning melted fat or juice over the meat during cooking time to keep it moist.

DEEP FRYING

Has a bit of a bad name. That's hardly surprising after the antics of those who decided this was a good way to cook Mars bars.

I maintain that, done properly, this is actually a quite healthy way to cook.

Just follow some golden rules:

Good quality clean fat must be used and changed regularly and not allowed to overheat.

It is best to use a thermostatically controlled fryer rather than a pan on the stove as there's always the danger it could catch fire.

There should be sufficient fat but never fill more than half to two-thirds full.

SHALLOW FRYING

Ask most people how many methods of shallow frying there are and I'll wager most will say one. There are in fact four:

Shallow Fry – the cooking of food in a small amount of fat or oil, typically fish, meat, eggs, pancakes and asparagus;

Sauté – this is when the food is tossed during cooking – widely-used for potatoes, onions and kidneys (sauté means to jump or toss). It's also employed in dishes like beef stroganoff where the meat is cooked first and then the sauce is made in the pan with the meat;

Griddle – foods cooked on a metal plate, for example, burger and sausages;

Stir-fry – stir frying is an Asian, particularly Chinese, method of cooking. Food for stir frying must be cut small before cooking and then placed into a hot wok a little at a time. It's a quick method of cooking, it keeps the food crisp and retains the nutritional values of the food. It's also a light and healthy way of cooking.

Always heat the wok first before adding any oil and make sure that all of the ingredients are ready to go as things happen fast.

BAKING

The mind immediately conjures up images of hot, crusty fresh bread straight from the oven. I can't decide what's best about it – the smell, the texture or the taste.

The same goes for seeing your pizza emerge from the glowing furnace of a wood-fired oven. It's simply mouth-watering. The intense heat of the oven gives the pizza a lovely crispy base.

STEAMING

Cooking by moist heat with varying degrees of pressure.

Low pressure steaming allows the food to make contact with the moist steam.

High pressure is a method in which the steam is not allowed to escape. The resulting build-up of pressure increases the temperature and reduces cooking time.

It's a very healthy way of cooking which maintains nutritional value and reduces the risk of over cooking.

SOUS-VIDE COOKING (UNDER VACUUM)

Very trendy within the chef world at the moment. It's the method of cooking food sealed in airtight plastic bags in a water bath for a long time – up to 72 hours in some cases.

It's cooked at a much lower temperature such as 60°C and the intention is to cook the food evenly, while keeping it moist. Sealing the food in plastic bags also keeps in juices and aroma that would otherwise be lost in the cooking process. The need for temperatures much lower than for conventional cooking is a defining feature of sous-vide.

HERBS
Unlimited

A passion for good food and the poor availability of quality fresh herbs inspired Alison Dodd to start growing her own herbs in Yorkshire.

Starting her career as a Cordon Bleu chef, she soon recognised the need for a good supply of fresh herbs to the catering industry.

Herbs Unlimited progressed from supplying local restaurants and hotels to supplying the catering trade throughout the North of England as well as businesses within the food processing sector.

Fresh herbs have been gradually rediscovered as a primary source of flavour, and with more concern about healthy eating, coupled with the desire to support local producers and reduce 'food miles', demand has continued to increase.

To further develop the business, Alison went into partnership with Thirsk-based farmer, Trevor Bosomworth. A new site was developed, which included two acres of polytunnels and glasshouses, a state of the art packhouse and 35 acres of field crops.

Says Alison: "We specialise in high-quality fresh cut herbs and baby salads. The polytunnels give us an extended season to grow our unique range of baby leaves and speciality herbs, and this is done to the highest specification using innovative growing methods and biological controls. Our dedicated growers are committed to producing crops in as natural and environmentally sensitive way as they can".

WILD GARLIC VELOUTE

(Serves 4)

Wild garlic or (Alliums ursinum as Alan Titchmarsh might say) grow in woodland, near or among bluebells. If you have ever walked through woodland in the spring and caught a blast of that garlic and onion smell then you can be sure there is wild garlic nearby. Either that, or you've stumbled on a curry house in the middle of the forest.

There is a notable resurgence of interest among chefs about foraging wild garlic, which can easily be found in woodland, semi-shaded areas and around river banks. Unlike the domestic version, it's the leaves on wild garlic rather than the bulbs that are prized. Although the bulbs can still be eaten they are a lot smaller than the shop-bought varieties and are slightly milder. The leaves can be eaten raw or made into a cracking pesto.

Ingredients

500g	washed wild garlic leaves
2	medium potatoes, washed peeled and diced
2	cloves garlic, crushed
	the green leaves of two leeks, washed and finely sliced
2	banana shallots, finely chopped
125ml	white wine
1 litre	chicken stock
100ml	double cream
25g	butter
	drizzle olive oil
	bouquet garni of thyme, bay leaves and parsley stalks
	chopped parsley
	salt and pepper

Method

For the confit potatoes:

Add half of the diced potatoes to a pan with a splash of olive oil, one clove of garlic and one sprig of thyme. Cook on a low heat until soft.

For the wild garlic veloute:

Heat a large pan. Add the olive oil, butter and melt.

Add the shallots, leeks, diced potato, garlic and bouquet garni to the oil and butter, and cook without colour for approximately 3-4 minutes or until soft.

Add the white wine and reduce by half. Add the chicken stock and bring slowly to the boil.

Turn the heat down and simmer until the potatoes are soft.

Add the cream and season with salt and pepper. Remove the bouquet garni. Add the wild garlic and stir into the liquid. Cook until wilted – about 2 minutes.

Blend in a food processor and pass through a fine sieve.

To serve, place a few confit potatoes into the bottom of a bowl and pour over the wild garlic veloute. A few wild garlic flowers can be placed on top of the soup.

BEETROOT SOUP

Rich and earthy, this humble root vegetable makes a great soup and deserves more than just being pickled.

Ingredients

	drizzle olive oil
1	medium onion, peeled and diced
1	medium carrot, peeled and diced
1	stick celery, chopped
6cm	piece white of leek
1kg or 8	large red beetroot, washed peeled and diced
12	baby beetroot
1 litre	vegetable stock
	bouquet garni of thyme
150ml	crème frâiche
	salt and pepper

Method

Heat a large heavy bottomed pan and add the olive oil. Add the onion, leek, celery and carrot and sweat until soft.

Add the bouquet garni of thyme and the diced beetroot and cook for a further 3-4 minutes.

Add the vegetable stock. Bring to the boil and then simmer for 15 minutes.

While the soup is cooking, in a separate pan boil the baby beetroot in boiling water and a little salt and cook until soft – approximately 10 minutes. You can tell when the beetroot is cooked as the skin will simply slip right off.

When the soup is ready (the diced beetroot should be soft) pour or ladle into a blender or food processor and whiz until smooth. Be careful as the soup is red hot.

Pass through a chinois or sieve into a clean pan to keep hot.

To serve, ladle into soup bowls and garnish with the baby beetroot and a spoonful of crème frâiche and a few thyme flowers if you are lucky enough to have them.

SPINACH, GOAT'S CHEESE AND ASPARAGUS TART

(Serves 4)

What a combination! Yorkshire asparagus from Sandhutton and creamy white goat's cheese a real winner.

Ingredients

¾	pint milk
100g	spinach
4	eggs
4	spring onions
200g	ricotta
12	spears asparagus
1 tbsp	parmesan
200g	goat's cheese
	pinch of nutmeg
50g	parmesan cheese
	pinch of salt
	pinch of baby thyme

For the pastry

500g	plain flour
125g	butter, cold & diced
125g	lard, diced
	cold water to bind
1	egg, beaten

Method

In a bowl crack the eggs, add the ricotta, nutmeg, parmesan, salt and carefully mix.

Gradually add the milk and whisk until combined, add a pinch of baby thyme and mix through. (This egg mixture can keep in the fridge for up to 4 days).

Add the washed spinach to the tart ring.

Add the sliced spring onion and crumble in the goat's cheese.

Carefully pour in the egg and ricotta mix.

Gently blanch the asparagus spears for 2-3 minutes then place the the tips on top of the tart.

Sprinkle on the thyme.

Carefully place in to the oven at 160ºC for 20 minutes, or until the egg and ricotta mix has set.

You can take the tart out just before the egg mix has set, as the heat will carry on cooking it when removed from the oven.

Allow to cool slightly before removing from the tin.

Serve with a crisp asparagus salad, a poached egg, or both.

For the pastry

In a large mixing bowl, add the cold diced butter and lard to the flour.

With your hands, gently rub together the combined mixture to a sandy texture.

Bring together by adding a tablespoon of cold water at a time while mixing.

Don't over work the pastry.

Line your tart cases and blind bake in the oven for 10-15 minutes. Remove and brush with a beaten egg, this will seal in the tart filling.

YORKSHIRE PUDDINGS

(Serves 4)

The story goes that this recipe was brought back to England by the crusaders, who told their wives about a wonderful French dish called soufflé they had tried en route to the holy land. They apparently listed the ingredients pretty accurately, but forgot to mention the bit about the amount of beating required. So the dish fell flat, but not in my part of the kingdom, where it's our 'national' dish. Approach it without fear – this recipe has never failed to rise to the occasion.

Ingredients

200g	plain flour
200g	eggs
100g	milk
100g	water
	pinch salt and ground white pepper
	knob of dripping

Method

All you have to do is use a cup or mug and fill each time with your ingredients.

e.g. cup of plain flour sieved, cup of milk and water – half and half, pinch of salt and pepper and whisk together.

Add a cup of eggs to the flour mix and whisk. Leave to rest.

At the Butchers Arms we make our Yorkshire pudding batter the night before and leave in the fridge (don't ask why, they just make a better Yorkshire pudding).

Remove the batter from the fridge and whisk again.

Heat your Yorkshire pudding trays with a knob of dripping and place in a hot oven for 15 minutes.

Carefully remove the now hot trays from the oven. The fat will be very hot, almost with a blue hazy smoke.

Add the batter to the Yorkshire pudding tins. The batter will sizzle as it hits the side of the tins. Fill to about three quarters full.

Place in the oven approximately 180°C and leave until well-risen and golden brown.

Tip: Don't open the oven door too early or the Yorkshire Puddings will fall flat.

AUTUMN MINESTRONE SOUP (Serves 4)

This is a great hearty soup and its jam-packed full of goodness and will do the world of good for anyone that eats it.

Soup is a great way to make the most of the seasons vary your choice of vegetables throughout the year and use what's best in that season

Ingredients

100g	onion peeled and chopped
100g	carrots washed peeled and chopped
100g	celery washed and chopped
100g	leek washed and chopped
100g	celeriac washed peeled and chopped
100g	butternut squash, washed peeled and chopped
50g	cabbage washed and shredded
1	clove garlic crushed
1 can	plum tomatoes
1 tsp	tomato purée
100g	haricot beans cooked
500ml	vegetable stock
	thyme, parsley
	drizzle olive oil

Method

Warm the pan on the stove.

Drizzle in the olive oil.

Add the onion, carrot, celery, and leek and gently cook without colour for a couple of minutes.

Add the celeriac and butternut squash and again cook without colour.

Add the garlic and stir in.

Add the pasta and tomato purée and chopped tomatoes.

Add the vegetable stock and bring to the boil.

Reduce the heat so that the soup is simmering.

Add the cabbage and haricot beans.

Bring back to the simmer correct the seasoning and add the thyme and chopped parsley and serve.

RED ONION TART TATIN WITH YELLISON FARM GOAT'S CHEESE

(Serves 4)

Ingredients

300g	puff pastry
4	red onions
100g	granulated sugar
75g	butter
10g	sugar
	pinch thyme leaves
	chopped rosemary leaves
200g	Yellison goat's cheese
1 tsp	beetroot finely diced
100ml	drizzle balsamic
	drizzle olive oil
	pinch salt & pepper
1 sprig	thyme
1	bay leaf

For the Soubise sauce:

25g	butter
400g	onions sliced thin
125ml	white wine
250g	cream
2	marjoram stalks
2	thyme stalks

Method

In a clean pan heat the sugar and 50g of butter to form a caramel.

Pour carefully into 4 tart tatin moulds.

Peel 2 red onions and slice in half and core. Place into the caramel.

Peel and slice the other 2 red onions and cook with a little butter in a medium pan, keep stirring occasionally, this will take about 20 minutes.

When almost cooked add the sugar, deglaze the caramelised onions with balsamic and reduce until the vinegar has gone. Season with salt and pepper.

Place a spoonful of the onion marmalade over the onions in the caramel.

Roll out the puff pastry to half cm thick and cut into 4 disks. Slightly larger than the tart tatin tins.

Place the pastry over the onions and gently tuck the pastry in.

Place in oven at 200ºC for about 30 minutes.

Remove and allow to cool slightly then turn out (be careful as the caramel is very hot) and add a pinch of thyme and rosemary.

Place the goat's cheese on top and place back in the oven to glaze the top of the goat's cheese. This should be lightly caramelised.

For the roast balsamic beetroot

In a hot pan add a little olive oil and then carefully place in the beetroot and toss a little. Then add thyme and bay leaf, season with salt and pepper.

Roast in the oven until almost done, remove and coat with the balsamic stir.

Place back into the oven to finish cooking, the balsamic should be sticky.

For the Soubise sauce

Sweat the onions in the butter without colour.

Add the thyme and marjoram stalks. Add the white wine and reduce by half, then cream and bring to the boil. Reduce until the sauce has thickened slightly.

Season with salt and pepper, then whizz until smooth with a hand blender. Pass through a fine sieve.

To serve

Place the goat's cheese tart tatin in the centre of the plate. Scatter the beetroot round the outside and dress with a little balsamic. Then spoon over the Soubise sauce.

Garnish with baby thyme, marjoram leaves and baby onion shoots.

CRISPY ROASTED BELLY PORK WITH PAN-SEARED KING SCALLOPS, BLACK PUDDING AND WAKEFIELD RHUBARB

(Serves 4)

This is a simple and great dish. The creaminess of the scallops, the earthy richness of the black pudding and the sharpness of the rhubarb go perfectly well together. Scallops can be bought in or out of their shells. Look out for scallops that have been harvested by hand-diving. This method has less impact on the environment than dredging for scallops.

Ingredients

1kg	belly pork
1tsp	crushed fennel seeds
	small pinch ground cloves
	Cornish sea salt
12	large scallops, prepared and cleaned
8 slices	local black pudding
6 stems	Wakefield forced rhubarb, 4 washed and chopped and 2 washed and cut into batons
50g	sugar
½	split vanilla pod
½	orange juice and zest
	rapeseed oil
50g	Yorkshire butter
	salt and pepper

Method

For the roast belly pork:

Preheat the oven to 200ºC. Using a very sharp knife or Stanley knife score the pork skin in parallel lines approximately ½cm apart.

Drizzle the rapeseed oil over the pork and rub in the fennel, cloves and sea salt, making sure that you rub into the scored skin.

Place the pork onto a rack in a roasting tin and pour 1 litre of boiling water into the roasting tin (this will stop the fat from burning and keep the pork meat moist and tender).

Roast for 30 minutes or until the pork skin is golden.

Turn the oven down to 160ºC and roast the pork for a further 2 hours. The juices should run clear when pricked with a fork and the skin should be deep golden and very crisp.

Remove from the oven and allow to rest for 20 minutes.

For the rhubarb:

In a saucepan, melt the sugar and orange juice and zest.

Add the chopped rhubarb and vanilla. Cover with a lid and simmer for 10-15 minutes. Remove the lid and blend until smooth.

Add the baton rhubarb and simmer a little faster for another 5 minutes. Set aside and keep warm.

For the black pudding and scallops:

In a frying pan heat a little rapeseed oil and add the black pudding. Fry until crispy, turn over and repeat on the other side. Remove from the pan and keep warm.

Place the cleaned seasoned scallops into the medium hot pan and sear in a little oil until golden brown. Turn them over and add a knob of butter (this will give the scallops a rich creamy flavour).

The scallops should be medium rare and warm in the middle. They should take about 5-6 minutes to cook, so don't overcook.

Place the warm rhubarb on the plate.

Place the black pudding on the plate and neatly arrange the scallops on top.

Slice the pork and arrange on the plate.

Drizzle with a garden herb dressing and garnish with micro salad and herbs.

WHEN THE
boat comes in...

Fish, out of all the food that I cook in my professional kitchen, is my ultimate favourite.

It doesn't matter what variety it is as long as it's in season. When my suppliers call me on a Tuesday to tell me what is coming off the boats that week, it's all I can do to stop myself ordering everything. I love cooking fish that much.

And the big secret is that it is so easy to cook.

As an island, Great Britain has an unlimited supply of fish and shell fish (well without going into the details of the fishing regulations) and as a chef it has always surprised me that we don't eat more of it.

We are so different from our European neighbours – like the Spanish, French and Italians – who eat far more fish and shellfish that we do.

I think that a lot of people are afraid to cook fish because they think it will be too difficult or it will make the house smell unpleasantly.

Fish are classified into six distinct categories:

Round	or	Flat
(cod, haddock, hake)		(plaice, Dover eyes and lemon sole, halibut)

Fresh	or	Salt
(fish from lakes and rivers)		(fish from the sea)

White	or	Oily
(cod, haddock, halibut)		(mackerel, herring, tuna)

Quality points to look out for when buying fresh fish:

Freshness is the key. If you are in a restaurant on a Monday, chances are that the fish on the menu was landed on Thursday and delivered to the restaurant on Friday or Saturday – and the fresh stock of fish will be delivered on Tuesday. So, I would stay clear of ordering it on a Monday.

Absolute freshness is essential and here are a few points to look out for:

• Eyes should be bright clear and plump. Eyes that are dull and sunken are a few days old;
• The gills should be bright red;
• Fish should smell of the sea – fresh and salty;
• Scales on fish should be plentiful and should not come off when rubbed;
• There should also be a covering of sea slime on healthy fish.

Everybody loves white fish – we can put cod loin or halibut on our menu and it will sell like hot cakes. But we have all heard about the pressures of overfishing and the depleting stocks of cod and haddock. So the next time you buy fish try more sustainable varieties like hake, coly, gurnard, pollock or whiting.

Different cuts of fish:

Steak (darne)   a slice of a round fish through the bone e.g. salmon

Steak (troncon)   a slice of flat fish through the bone e.g. turbot

Delice   a piece of fish neatly folded, usually sole

Goujon   let's be honest – it's a posh name for a fish finger

Paupiette   small fillets of plaice or sole stuffed with a mousse and rolled neatly

Shellfish fall into three categories:

Crustaceans   lobsters, crabs, crayfish, langoustines and prawns

Molluscs   bi-valves have two shells – mussels, clams, scallops and oysters whereas
                         univalves have one (eg whelks and winkles)

Cephalopods   squid, also known as calamari, is probably the best known,
                         but there's also cuttlefish and octopus

All shellfish should be bought live to ensure freshness and cooked on the same day of purchase.

TAKING UP SMOKING WITH JUSTIN STAAL AT STAAL SMOKEHOUSE

It's always a source of pleasure to me when I discover great Yorkshire food producers and Justin is most certainly one of those.

He describes his art in the following way;

"The curing and smoking of meat, game and fish is an age-old form of food preservation. For us this traditional process is still one the best ways of producing some of the most wonderful, mouth-watering foods available. It is a slow process and great care needs to be taken at every step to ensure the end product is of the finest quality.

The first step in our smoking process is to start off with high quality, fresh produce. At Staal Smokehouse, we source almost all of ours from selected local farms, the only exception being Atlantic salmon. This comes from the cold, clean waters off the west coast of Scotland. For me, it's still the best salmon you can find anywhere.

Our fish are dry-cured with sea salt and dark molasses sugar. After curing we give the products time to mature. This allows the salt to disperse evenly through the flesh, initiating a chemical change that enhances the flavour and appearance of the end product. It also allows the next key ingredient to work its magic – the smoke.

The produce is placed in a locally-built kiln where a blend of oak and apple wood sawdust is allowed to smoulder, generating a fine smoke that is drawn over the fish. Most is cold-smoked, but we also use the alternative method of hot smoking, raising the temperature so that the salmon is roasted in the kiln.

From the kiln our smoked products are taken into the chiller and allowed to mature a little longer. This allows the smoke to disperse evenly through the fish and gives our products their wonderful texture and taste."

BEETROOT-POACHED SCOTTISH SALMON WITH WOK-FRIED ASIAN GREENS AND NOODLES

(Serves 4)

Quick light and fresh, a great supper dish with that little oriental feel.

Ingredients

4	180g salmon fillets skinned
250ml	beetroot juice
	drizzle sesame seed oil
1	medium red onion
2cm	fresh ginger
1	red chilli (seeds removed)
4	heads of pak choi
100g	soft noodles (pre-cooked)
	pinch coriander
25g	beetroot (julienne, thin strips)
100ml	chilli jam

Method

In a pan add the beetroot juice and bring to the boil and then reduce the heat to approximately 95°C.

Add the salmon to the beetroot juice and poach for approximately 10 minutes.

In a wok add the sesame seed oil and red onion, ginger and chilli and toss together in the pan.

Add the pak choi stalks and then the noodles allowing the noodles to warm through.

Add the pak choi leaves, coriander and beetroot and a touch of salt.

Arrange on the plate and dress with a drizzle of chilli jam.

BAKED SCALLOPS IN THE SHELL

(Serves 4)

Ingredients

8	scallops
2	egg yolks
2 tbsp	olive oil
2	shallots
2	carrots
1	leek
100g	spinach
2cm	ginger
½	chilli
	a pinch of fine herbs (chives, dill, coriander and chervil)
	splash of white wine
	salt and pepper to taste
	toasted sesame seed oil

Method

Roll out the puff pastry as thin as possible to 30x20cm rectangle.

Place the pastry on a chopping board and brush with the egg yolk and a little water and place in the fridge.

Shuck the scallops (keep the shells) and remove the skirt. Gently wash the scallops to remove any grit and sand, pat dry with a tea towel.

Preheat the oven to 200ºC.

Pick the spinach to remove the stalk (baby spinach is best). Peel the carrot and using a mandolin cut into spaghetti. Wash and peel the leek and using the white and the green part cut finely into spaghetti. Peel and slice the shallots and blanch the carrots, leek and shallots for around 1 minute. Peel and slice the ginger and cut into matchsticks.

Wash and scrub the scallop shells in hot soapy water, rinse and dry well.

Place the spinach into the curved half of the shell add 2 scallops then add the blanched carrot, leek, shallot, ginger and chilli.

Season lightly and drizzle with olive oil and a splash of white wine (Chablis would be my preference) then place the flat scallop lid on top.

Remove the pastry from the fridge and cut a strip lengthways about 2.5cm wide. Make sure the egg washed side is against the scallop shell. Use the pastry to seal the two shells together and repeat until all 4 shells are filled and sealed.

Place the scallop shells onto a baking tray, egg wash once more and cook for ten minutes or until the pastry is golden.

Serve the scallops in the shells with some crusty bread.

CRISPY GRILLED PRAWNS WITH TB's GROWN UP TOMATO KETCHUP

(Serves 4)

We serve this as a trio at The Butchers Arms but they are great just on their own too. There is something so satisfying about peeling prawns and savouring the sweet juices!

Ingredients

1	skewer
2	large prawns
	drizzle olive oil
1 tbsp	tomato ketchup (See basic recipes)
	splash of Tabasco
1	garlic clove, crushed
	touch of grated nutmeg
	splash of Henderson's Relish
1/2 tsp	Dijon mustard
I	small piece red chilli, deseeded and diced
	pinch of baby coriander

Method

In a bowl make the marinade by combining the garlic, chilli, olive oil, mustard, Henderson's Relish, ketchup and nutmeg.

Skewer the prawns and place in the marinade for 12 hours.

Griddle on a hot stove until crispy and slightly coloured, turn over and repeat.

Serve with a little of the warmed marinade and dress with baby coriander.

This makes an ideal partner to an oriental dish, for instance, Tempura Oyster Samphire.

Tempura Oyster, Samphire *(Serves 4)* and Lemon Beurre Blanc

Ingredients

100g	cornflour
200g	self-raising flour
1	egg yolk
350ml	iced carbonated water
1	oyster, opened, juice saved and bottom shell washed
25g	samphire
5g	butter

Method

Sieve the cornflour and self-raising flour into a bowl, add the egg yolk and lightly whisk in the iced water.

Dip the oyster in the butter and deep fry at 180°C until crispy, then drain.

In a pan, add the butter then add the washed samphire and sauté for 1 minute.

Add two spoons of lemon beurre blanc and warm.

Place the shell on the plate with all the samphire and lemon beurre blanc, then place the tempura oyster on top.

You can also try this with a crab claw.

GRILLED FORTUNES OF WHITBY KIPPERS WITH BUTTER, LEMON AND BABY PICKERING WATERCRESS

(Serves 4)

Kippers are herrings which are split open through the back to the belly then cured and cold smoked. In my view, there is no finer example of this most intensely-flavoured delicacy than those smoked in the traditional way by Fortunes in Whitby, that mecca for lovers of good seafood. Kippering is an old name for salting and cold smoking. This is a great late breakfast or early lunchtime meal and so simple.
There is little to compare with the pleasure of tucking into a freshly-smoked kipper while taking in the sea views on the beautiful North Yorkshire coast around Whitby.

Ingredients

1	Fortunes smoked kipper
	butter
	lemon
	baby watercress
	lemon wedge
	brown bread

Method

Pre-heat the grill.

Place the kipper on a tray skin side down. Place the butter on the kipper and squeeze on the lemon juice.

Grill under a moderate heat.

The kipper is cooked when the bone removes away from the flesh.

Serve with the lemon wedge and brown bread.

HOT SMOKED SALMON, SOFT-BOILED HEN'S EGG, SAFFRON MAYONNAISE, CUCUMBER & BABY SALAD

(Serves 4)

The Salmon is smoked in two ways, Hot Smoked or Cold Smoked.
Hot smoking cooks the fish because it is smoked over heat for 6-12 hours. Cold smoked fish is firstly cured in dry salt or brine then smoked at a much lower temperature for 24 to 48 hours.

Ingredients

600g	fresh salmon
	good handful of oak chippings
4	eggs
	half a cucumber
100ml	mayonnaise
	pinch saffron soaked in a little white wine
	handful of baby chervil, dill, celery leaf
	sea salt

Method

For the salmon

Place the oak chips on the bottom of a smoking tin and heat over the gas stove. When smoking place the salmon onto the rack and place the lid on top. Smoke for about 10-12 minutes, turn off the gas and allow the salmon to rest in the smoking tin.

For the eggs

Place the eggs into boiling water, boil for 5 minutes, refresh immediately. Remove the shells carefully.

Reheat when required for 30 seconds in boiling salted water.

Trim the bottom and remove the top with a spoon exposing the yolk.

For the saffron mayonnaise

Use the soaked saffron strands which will have released the rich colour. Mix in with a little of the mayonnaise, which should give a rich golden mayonnaise.

For the cucumber

Peel and, using a parisienne scoop, scoop out cucumber balls. Set to one side.

To assemble the dish

Remove the salmon from the smoker and flake the fish into big flakes.

Dab a spoon of saffron mayonnaise onto one side of the plate and smudge with the back of the spoon. On the other side of the plate place the flaked salmon down one side.

Place the warm egg next to the salmon and garnish with the cucumber and baby chervil, dill, celery leaf and Cornish sea salt.

LINGUINE ALLE VONGOLE

In Italy, recipes for linguine alle vongole vary from region to region and even restaurant to restaurant – with each one claiming that their recipe is the best! Some will add fresh chilli, some will add dried chilli flakes, and even, on occasion, I have seen fresh chopped tomatoes added. But the best and simplest I ever tasted was on the Amalfi coast in the swish resort of Positano. There I found a handful of seafood restaurants that specialised in good fresh food simply cooked from the day's catch. Bellisimma!

Ingredients

400g	linguine or spaghetti
	good glug Tuscan virgin olive oil
2	shallots, finely chopped
4	cloves chopped garlic
1	deseeded and chopped red chilli
1kg	fresh clams in shell
	small handful flat leaf Italian parsley, chopped
	glass dry white wine
	half a lemon, juiced
	knob unsalted butter
	fresh ground black pepper

Method

Cook the pasta in plenty of boiling salted water to which you have added a little olive oil. The linguine will take about 6-7 minutes.

While the pasta is cooking, heat the olive oil in a large pan big enough to hold the clams, and gently fry the shallots, garlic and chilli.

Place the clams to the hot pan along with the white wine and lemon juice, cover with a lid and give the pan a little shake – this will help the clams to open.

Cook for 4-5 minutes shaking the pan occasionally until the clams have opened.

Add the butter and chopped parsley with the drained linguine and stir over a low heat and serve.

MACKEREL ON TOAST WITH SALTED CUCUMBER AND HORSERADISH

(Serves 4)

Ingredients

For the pickling juice

200g	sugar
50g	salt
500ml	white wine vinegar
1 litre	water
5	shallots, peeled and sliced
1 tsp	peppercorns
2	star anise
	few stalks of parsley and dill
	sprig of thyme
	olive oil

For the salted cucumber and horseradish

	half a cucumber, peeled and thinly sliced on a mandolin
	salt
4 tbsp	grated fresh horseradish
2 tbsp	crème frâiche
2 tsp	English mustard powder
4	fresh mackerel fillets
	salt and freshly ground black pepper
	knob of butter
4	slices soda bread, toasted and buttered
1	small red onion, thinly sliced
1/2	a small lemon

Method

For the pickling juice

In a pan, lightly sweat the shallots in a little olive oil (this is to take the edge off the shallots).

Add the rest of the pickling juice ingredients and bring to a gentle simmer.

Pour this hot pickling juice over the mackerel as the acidity of the juice along with the heat will gently cook the fish. Cover the tray and allow to cool.

For the salted cucumber and horseradish

Place the cucumber slices in a colander and sprinkle with plenty of salt. Mix well and leave the contents to drain over the sink for half an hour.

Rinse the salt off the cucumber with cold water, then leave to drain. Gently wring out any excess moisture from the cucumber with your hands, and then set aside.

In a clean bowl, mix the horseradish with the crème frâiche and mustard powder, making sure the mustard powder is well combined with no lumps. Set aside.

Season the mackerel fillets on their skin side with salt and freshly ground black pepper.

Heat the butter in a frying pan until it is foaming and then add the fillets skin-side down. Place a heatproof plate on the cooking fillets, as this will make sure they stay flat and cook evenly. Fry for 4-5 minutes or until nearly cooked through, then turn the fillets and cook for 30 seconds, or until just cooked through.

To serve

Place a small handful of cucumber on the toast. Place the pickled mackerel fillets on the cucumber. Top with a dollop of the horseradish sauce and garnish with a little of the sliced red onion and a squeeze of lemon.

MUSSELS A LA MARINIERE

(Serves 4)

I have fond memories of my great-grandfather coming back with mussels he had collected. He'd heap them on the coal shovel and place it straight onto the fire. Whatever way you enjoy them, mussels in season are a delight. Here's the classic take on cooking them.

Ingredients

1kg	mussels
150ml	white wine
2	shallots peeled and sliced
2	sticks celery
100g	samphire
150ml	whipped cream
	good pinch chopped flat leaf parsley
25g	butter

Method

Prepare the mussels by washing them in cold running water and remove the beards and barnacles. Place into a bowl.

Heat a large pan with a lid on it. Add the butter and sweat the shallots and celery without colour, then add the garlic and cook for another minute. Add the mussels and white wine, place the lid on top of the pan, gently shake the pan (this will aggravate the mussels to open them.)

Cook for appoximately 5 minutes until the mussels have opened.

Add the cream, samphire and chopped parsley and bring to the boil once more. Spoon out into 4 bowls and pour over the cream sauce.

Serve with crusty bread.

NORTH SEA FISH AND SHELLFISH STEW

This works well with any fish you can get your hands on, so don't worry if you cannot get all the varieties in the list. Just ask your friendly fishmonger to suggest some alternatives.

Ingredients

200ml	olive oil
8	marinated anchovies
2	large shallots, finely chopped
4	cloves garlic
1	bulb fennel
12	roasted plum tomatoes, seeds removed
200g	tomato purée
2	sticks celery
1	small leek
1	carrot
6	sprigs thyme, tied together
2	bay leaves
200ml	dry white wine
50ml	Pernod
	pinch saffron
500ml	fish stock
1	lemon
250ml	double cream
	handful parsley, chopped
1	whole lobster, cooked and shell removed
8	langoustines, tails and shell removed
300g	clams, scrubbed
300g	mussels, scrubbed
4	oysters, shucked (keep the juice)
4	scallops, cleaned
500g	each of hake, gurnard, pollock, John Dory, seabass and red mullet, scaled and pin-boned.

Method

In a jar, soak the saffron in a little of the white wine.

Heat olive oil in a large pan then add the shallots, garlic, fennel, celery, leek and carrot, and fry gently for 10-12 minutes until soft without colour.

Stir in the anchovies, bay, thyme and parsley, and cook for a further 2 minutes.

Add the tomato purée and roasted tomatoes, followed by the Pernod and white wine. Reduce the liquid by half.

Stir in the fish stock and bring to the boil. Pour in the cream and bring back to the boil.

Sear the fish in a hot pan for a minute or two so that the outside crisps up but the fish is not cooked all the way through. Meanwhile place the shellfish in the pan containing the sauce mixture, simmer for 4-5 minutes and then add the fish.

Cook until the clams and mussels have opened.

Check the seasoning (the clams, mussels and oysters plus the juice should give the stew a slightly salty fresh taste).

Remove the thyme bunch. Add the chopped parsley and juice of the lemon and stir in carefully.

Serve straight from the pot with crusty bread and aioli.

North Sea Fish Pie

(Serves 4)

The best comfort food! You can add spinach, peas, hardboiled egg, smoked salmon to the fish pie recipe. Grated cheddar cheese on top.

Ingredients

100g	butter
100g	flour
1 litre	fish stock (See basic recipes)
	pinch of parsley
200ml	cream
150g	hake, cubed, skinned and de-boned
150g	pollock, cubed, skinned and de-boned
150g	smoked haddock, cubed, skinned and de-boned
8	langoustines
4	crab claws
1	lobster tail, sliced into escallops

For the mashed potatoes

1kg	potatoes, washed, peeled and quartered
	pinch of salt & pepper
50g	unsalted butter
150ml	warm cream

Method

For the veloute

Melt the 50g butter in a pan add the flour and mix to a roux, cook this gently for about 4 minutes, heat the fish stock and gradually add to the roux a ladle at a time until you have a smooth sauce. Cover with cling film and move to one side.

Add the cream to this veloute and simmer.

Check the seasoning in the sauce.

Place the cubed hake, pollock and smoked haddock in to the veloute and fold gently through the sauce.

Add the freshly chopped parsley and spoon into dish.

For the mashed potatoes

Place the potatoes and a pinch of salt into a pan and cover with cold water.

Bring to the boil and cook for about 15-20 minutes or until the potatoes are tender.

Drain in a colander (let the steam dry the potatoes out a little).

Return to the pan and mash until smooth, add the butter and warm cream, then mix until smooth.

Season with salt and pepper.

For the fish pie

Add the lobster tail evenly on top (you do not want it all to go onto one spoon when dishing out).

Place mashed potato into piping bag with star nozzle and pipe on top of the fish, you can place carefully on top and use a fork to prick up the mash but piping makes the finished dish look better.

Add the crab claw and langoustines body.

Place into a hot oven for appoximately 20 minutes or until the potato turns golden.

Remove from the oven and serve.

North Sea Hake Fillet with Wood Roast Peppers wilted Spinach and fresh Basil Pesto
(Serves 4)

Wood-fired peppers add a quite rustic and earthy note to the pronounced meaty flavour of the fish

Ingredients

4	200g Hake fillets, scaled and pin boned
1	roasted red Romano pepper diced
1	roasted yellow pepper diced
½	medium onion peeled and diced
1	clove garlic crushed
100g	washed spinach
25g	butter
	drizzle olive oil
	salt and pepper
	basil pesto (See basic recipes)

Method

Heat the olive oil in a pan, add the onion and cook without colour.

Add the garlic and the peppers and cook slowly.

In a sautéed pan heat and add the olive oil and half the butter season the Hake and fry skin side down until the skin is crisp.

Turn the fish over gently and cook gently.

Remove the Hake and allow to rest.

In the same pan add the rest of the butter and wilt the spinach season with salt and pepper.

Place the peppers and spinach on to a plate place the Hake on top drizzle the pesto round the outside and serve.

Garnish with baby water cress.

PAELLA OF FISH AND SEAFOOD

(Serves 4)

We normally have this dish when I come back from holiday, just to escape for a moment with the idea we're still sunning ourselves by the pool rather than watching the rain through the windows.

Ingredients

300g	paella rice (Arborio rice or short grain rice work just as good)
	drizzle extra virgin olive oil
1	Spanish onion finely diced
1	clove of garlic crushed
100g	Yorkshire chorizo diced
4	plum tomatoes, skinned, deseeded and chopped
½	Romario pepper diced into 1cm
	pinch saffron soaked in 100ml white wine
	salt and pepper
2 litres	fish stock
	pinch paprika
	pinch baby thyme
1	bay leaf
4	large king prawns split in half
4	king scallops cut in half
100g	Palourde clams or Amandes clams
200g	mussels cleaned
100g	prepared squid cut into rings
150g	cod
150g	halibut
150g	monkfish
	pinch flat leaf parsley
1	lemon cut into 4
	drizzle lemon oil

Method

In a paella pan or a large frying pan heat and then add the oil.

Add the diced onion and cook without colour then add the garlic, pepper and chorizo and cook gently until the chorizo starts to weep oil.

Stir in the paprika.

Now add the rice and stir in the pan until the rice is coated in the oil (the rice should look nice and glossy).

Add the white wine and saffron reduce by half.

Now add a ladle at a time of the simmering fish stock and stir this into the rice.

In a separate pan seal all the fish and keep to one side. (I know that this is not the traditional way to make paella but the result and finished dish will look great).

Keep adding a ladle at a time of the fish stock to the rice until there is about 1 litre of fish stock left, check the seasoning.

At this stage add the mussels and clams with the hinge pointing down into the rice (this will allow the clams and mussels to open).

Add the squid, fish, scallops and prawns and gently fold into the rice, add the rest of the fish stock and allow the rice to simmer gently.

The rice will be cooked when all of the fish stock has been absorbed by the rice.

Add the tomato, chopped parsley and lemon wedges and serve with four plates and a large serving spoon.

Pan-cooked Plaice with Clams, Lemon and Parsley Butter

(Serves 4)

This is a simple and great dish. There is something about cooking fish on the bone, it just tastes better and keeps the fish lovely and moist. Sometimes people are just a little scared of eating fish on the bone. When cooking fish on the bone try not to cook it too fast, a nice gentle approach will keep the fish moist.

Ingredients

2	whole plaice filleted

For the sauce

25g	plain flour
150g	clams
	pinch of Cornish sea salt
300ml	dry white wine
	pinch of ground white pepper
2	shallots finely chopped
	glug of olive oil
100g	cold diced butter
25g	butter
½	lemon juiced
50g	capers
	pinch of chopped parsley

Method

Place the flour, salt and pepper onto a tray and mix together.

Add the fish and coat well shaking off any excess flour. Heat the olive oil in a pan large enough for the plaice.

Place the plaice fillets into the hot oil but be careful that the oil does not splash. Slightly shake the pan to stop the plaice fillets from sticking. Cook for approximately 3 minutes then turn the whole fish over and cook on the other side for 3 minutes adding the butter at this point.

Once cooked (to check this, gently push the fish and see if it flakes slightly) the fish can then be placed into the oven at 120°C and left in the oven to finish cooking and rest for no longer than 5 minutes.

For the sauce

Sweat the shallots in a little butter without letting them colour. Add the white wine and clams, cover then allow to steam, these are cooked when open. Remove from the heat and gently whisk in the diced butter, lemon juice and herbs allowing the sauce to warm slightly.

Remove the dabs from the oven and place on warm plates. Spoon over the sauce and served with a simple lemon dressed salad.

WHITEBAIT

Whitebait are young immature sprats, most commonly herring, but can be sardines and mackerel. Such young fish often travel together in schools along the coast and move into estuaries. Whitebait are very tender therefore the entire fish is eaten including head, fins, bone and gut. They are hard to find fresh as they are normally frozen at sea.
Here's a great quick recipe.

Ingredients

400g	whitebait
250ml	milk
100g	flour to coat the whitebait
	lemon juice
	vegetable oil for deep frying
	pinch of Cornish sea salt
	pinch of cayenne pepper

wild garlic mayonnaise (See basic recipes) then just add a handful of chopped wild garlic leaves.

Method

Wash the whitebait in cold water and drain. Place in a bowl and cover with the milk. Remove the whitebait and pass through the flour. Shake well in a sieve to remove excess flour.

Place in a frying basket and plunge into hot oil. Fry quickly until crisp and golden brown. Shake the basket to prevent the whitebait from sticking, remove the whitebait from the frying basket and place onto kitchen paper.

Season with Cornish sea salt and cayenne pepper and serve with a good wedge of lemon and garlic mayonnaise.

SMOKING HADDOCK IN THE MIST

This dish is our take on smoked haddock chowder.

Ingredients

32	clams
400g	smoked east coast haddock
25g	butter
50g	smoked streaky bacon (optional)
110g	diced onion
300ml	milk
250g	potato diced, not washed
120ml	double cream
1	garlic clove, smashed
1	bouquet garni with some parsley stalks, a bay leaf and a sprig of thyme
	cooking liquor from the clams
	pinch of salt and ground white pepper
	chopped parsley
	smashed water biscuits

Method

Wash and scrub the clams and set to one side. Heat a large pan of water and bring to the boil. Place the clams in the water with a glass of white wine. Cover tightly with a lid and shake the pan a little to ensure the clams cook evenly. Once they have opened, remove from the heat. Drain in a colander and save the cooking liquor in a bowl. When they are cooled enough to handle remove the clam meat.

Melt the butter in a pan and fry the bacon (if using bacon) until brown. Add the onion and cook without colouring or until soft.

Place the milk in a separate pan with the bouquet garni and garlic clove and add the natural smoked haddock and bring to the boil. Turn down the heat and simmer for approximately 3 minutes.

Remove the haddock from the pan and set to one side to cool. Remove the garlic clove and bouquet garni. Add the unwashed diced potatoes and cream to the milk and bring to the boil. Reduce to a slow simmer until the potatoes have just cooked but are still firm (the reason for not washing the potatoes is that the starch will slightly thicken the milk).

Add the onion, bacon and clam cooking liquor and simmer for a further 5 minutes.

Add the clam meat and smoked haddock flaked slightly, taking care to remove any bones.

Simmer for a further 5 minutes.

Add the chopped parsley and season with salt if necessary and ground white pepper.

Serve with water biscuits.

DOWN ON
The Farm

BEEF

It's in the bag – most of the beef that's on the market today, that is.

Commercial meat producers seal beef within 24 hours of slaughter in a vacuum plastic bag, where it stays for between a week and 38 days in order to age. While this may preserve some of the essential qualities of the meat, it disappoints on the most important one of all – flavour. It just doesn't taste as good as beef which has been dry-aged.

In common with other chefs I've worked with, I believe the job has to be about more than standing around cooking in a kitchen. It means knowing about the food, where it comes from and how it's been reared and cared for.

Find the right quality product and in my view the less a chef does to it, the better. Over-complicate the dish and it's been a waste of the 18 months it's taken to get from pasture to plate.

I much prefer air-dried beef, with its characteristic deep burgundy colour and creamy yellow fat. It's quite easy to distinguish it from the bright red colour of meat on sale in many supermarkets. But there's much more about this wonderful versatile meat than just that.

So now let's go back to basics, since that's what this book is all about, and look at the language of beef. If you've ever wondered what all those names of cuts are about, here's your guide.

Cuts of Beef

The Fillet: Some say the most prized cut of beef, extremely tender and suits quick cooking. It is very lean with almost no fat and sits on the opposite side of the back to the sirloin. The fillet does very little work so is very tender, in fact the only work that the fillet does for the cow is to arch the back. So it has very little flavour and needs to benefit from good hanging. Being so tender makes it ideal for serving rare, blue or even tartare (a completely raw dish of prime fillet steak chopped and served with a hen's egg, shallots, capers, gherkins and mustard) or Carpaccio (an almost raw fillet, quickly sealed on the outside and sliced very thin).

The Sirloin: A prime cut from the lower middle of the back. Prepared on or off the bone for roasting, sirloin steaks or entrecote. The cut on the bone with the fillet is known as the T-bone.

The sirloin is mostly used as a premium steak. Should display good marbling and a thorough covering of fat on the outside. It needs to be hung well to develop flavour and help with the tenderisation.

Sirloin is an easy bet for home roast and is great served cold.

The Rib of Beef or Fore Rib: Located between the shoulder and the middle back, it has great proportions of inter-muscular fat which when correctly aged result in fantastic flavour and textures. Undoubtedly a prime cut and worth every penny.

When fully trimmed back to the main muscle eye (this is easily done) it can almost be pulled apart without a knife. When prepared like this the result is one of the best steaks ever – the rib eye.

As a roast there is none in my opinion better than the rib eye roll or, on the bone, the fore rib. It's more difficult to cook than the sirloin and is best served medium as opposed to rare. If you prefer your steak a bit more on the rare side, go for the sirloin.

We use this joint all the time in our pubs and restaurants for roasting on a Sunday, or off the bone for our rib eye steak.

The Featherblade or Flat Iron Steak: This cut sits on the side of the shoulder blade and when sliced looks like a feather.

Cut like this it is absolutely great for braising, however, if the nerve is removed it gives two great flat muscles that are lean and packed full of flavour. Flash-fried and served medium rare, this is one of the best steaks you can get.

The Brisket: A cut from the breast area. Typically boned and rolled, trimmed of excess fat and braised for a long period of time, it becomes almost butter-like. Brisket is a popular choice for salt or pickled beef.

The Topside: Cut from the hind quarter. An economical joint of more than acceptable quality when prepared correctly. A lean cut with reasonable texture and flavour which can be used for braising, minute steaks and for curing as in salt beef or the Italian Bresola (air dried beef).

Topside is a lean meat and can dry out easily so roast with plenty or vegetables and water in the roasting tray.

The Shin: One of my favourite cuts of beef especially cut on the bone. It needs slow moist cooking and has a lot of nerve and connective tissue. But when correctly cooked, results in tender, glutinous and flavoursome meat.

The Rump: Located at the base of the spine where the back joins on to the leg. This cut is made up of a few muscles. This is a full-flavoured steak when properly matured. The cheapest of the prime steaks.

The Oxtail: What a great cut. Cook this really slowly with root vegetables and red wine, and watch the meat fall of the bone – real comfort food.

VEAL

Veal is the Roman word for calf – and the Italians love it. It comes from male calves and the palest meat is thought to be the best. The meat darkens as the animals get older. Veal is a tender meat requiring little cooking, but the British eat less of it in comparison to pork and lamb.

PORK

Every part of the pig can be eaten except the squeal!

There are signs of quality in pork that you should look for: the flesh should be a pale pink colour, firm and a fine texture, and the fat should be white, firm, smooth and well propertied to the meat.

Free range organic or rare breed pork will have a deeper pink colour than the mass produced pork and these will have a far better taste. These pigs take longer to mature and this means that the end pig will be more expensive but the difference in taste is so much better.

The pork or bacon from traditional breeds carry extra fat and therefore keep the meat moist whilst cooking.

Rare Breeds include:
British Saddleback
Gloucestershire Old Spot
Large Back
Middle White
Tamworth
Pietrain

GREEDY LITTLE PIG

All our pork comes from the Greedy Little Pig hog roasting company, which is situated on a farm high above Holmfirth. Owner Carl Slingsby has a huge passion for all things pig. The breeding stock is Gloucestershire Old Spot as they make excellent mothers and have a good temperament and they use pure bread Pietrain as the bore as this gives excellent results when crossed with the Gloucestershire Old Spot.

Carl's biggest passion though is his cured air dried anything pig. Be it bacon, chorizo, salami, coppa ham, you name it, Carl can do it. He worked in France and Italy where he learned the trade and his cured meats are second to none. They are always on my menu. Carl's passion for charcuterie came about thanks to Hugh Fearnly-Whittingstall, having attended one of his courses at the River Cottage HQ in Dorset.

They also make their own Bresaola, which is a regional Italian speciality of cured beef fillet from Lombardy. But Carl from the Greedy Little Pig has perfected it here in the riding of west Yorkshire. The beef is traditionally cured in salt and then air-dried for several months during this time becomes deep red in colour. At The Butchers Arms we simply serve it sliced very thin with good virgin olive oil and a squeeze of lemon.

LAMB

OK, fastest finger on the buzzer. What was the name of the farmer in the film "Babe"?

Correct, Farmer Hogget! Now for a bonus point: what is a hogget?

What's that? No, I'm sorry, it is nothing to do with hogs. It's a sheep.

Lamb is called lamb when it is from an animal under a year old. After that it becomes hogget. So hogget is the name for the lamb that is over a year old. Mutton is a yet older sheep, generally over 18 months. The meat from each is cheaper than spring lamb.

Hogget has a stronger flavour than spring lamb but is prepared in much the same way, as the meat is not yet toughened. Most of our mutton comes from breeding animals that have reached the end of their productive contribution to the flock.

Early season lamb is a very tender meat with a pronounced flavour, which varies depending on where the sheep are raised and fed. Look for pale pink flesh in young animals and light to dark red in older animals.

When buying lamb, choose the leanest cuts with firm, creamy white fat. Rare breed lamb is farmed non-intensively and the flavour is much richer. You can buy named pure breed and rare breeds from good butchers. It costs a little more but the difference in flavour will be very noticeable. Rare breeds include Hebridean, Cotswold, Dorset Down, Oxford Down, Wensleydale, Swaledale and Rough Fell.

Lamb works well with a large range of accompaniments far beyond mint sauce. Generally the intense flavour of autumn lamb is a good match with equally strong seasonings and aromatic spices, for example, cumin. Or use garlic and rosemary to stud the skin before roasting a leg of lamb.

We use the whole carcass of lamb for the whole range of cooking methods including braising, roasting, shallow frying and grilling.

GAME

My fellow chef and Yorkshireman David Baldwin once delivered a now famous reply to a picky customer's complaint.

Given his noted quick wit, she should have known better than to hail him across the dining room.

"Mr Baldwin," she barked. "My pheasant has a piece of shot in it."

The reply came without hesitation: "Well it didn't ******* well die of old age, luv!"

It's true, when game is mentioned, thoughts of shotgun-toting tweed-clad gents roaming the moors for a bit of pheasant bagging come to mind.

But game is now, while not quite a mass-market item, readily accessible. Some types of game – for example, pheasants – are reared artificially and released into the wild to increase the stock, and the commercial farming of deer has proved highly successful, with the venison exhibiting a consistent flavour throughout the year. Yorkshire-based Round Green Farm is an outstanding example of such a producer.

Game of whatever type has a stronger flavour than farmed meats.

This is mainly due to the natural diet of grasses, grubs, berries and leaves. The meat is generally lean with little fat (except for wild duck).

All game should normally be hung for a time; the length of time depends on the type of game and the preference of the consumer. Hanging allows the flesh to tenderise and develop the characteristic "gamey" flavour.

Note that the supply of game is in many cases determined by the shooting season.

Here's Bilton's quick guide to the wild bunch:

Pheasant – one of the most handsome and popular of the game birds. It's usual to buy them by the brace with one cock and one hen. The season for pheasants is from October 1 to February 1.

Pigeon – a bird with dark flesh and a strong flavour. The season for pigeons is all year round.

Grouse – everyone thinks of the Glorious 12th when they think of grouse. It's tender when roasted and has a distinctive "wild bird" flavour. The season runs from August 12 to December 15.

Wild duck – duck includes Mallard, Widgeon and Teal. The season runs from September 1 to February 1.

Venison – hunting for wild deer is regulated by law.

Rabbit – a delicate flavour, similar to chicken. Always smell the meat to make sure it's fresh and sweet – and the body should be plump. Catch your rabbits all year round.

Hare – whereas rabbit has whitish flesh, hare is dark with a strong gamey flavour which gets stronger the longer it's hung. The season for hare is from August 1 to February 23.

POULTRY

The most important aspect of chicken for a chef is flavour.

Free range, organic and corn fed chickens are killed at twelve weeks while mass produced chickens are killed at six, so you have to consider that the extra six weeks that a chicken spends scratching round eating herbs is going to build up the flavour of the meat.

Our chickens and turkeys come from Herb-Fed Poultry, near York, and they are the best I've ever tasted. Owner Edward Wilkinson qualified as a chartered surveyor and after two years in London came home as a result of the credit crunch. With a family background in agriculture, Edward wanted to develop a food business in his home county of North Yorkshire. He approached a farming friend with the idea of rearing turkeys for Christmas as it was apparent there were few quality producers in the area.

At the same time Edward's aunt Alison Dodd was feeding her chickens on fresh herbs. She gave any surplus eggs to friends and neighbours and they were often praised as the best they had ever eaten.

Edward thought that if these herbs were having such an impact on an egg then what about a turkey – a bird that has gained a reputation for being dry and tasteless?

Edward took delivery of a trial batch of 500 bronze turkeys to test what would happen when they were fed on fresh herbs – and the results were fantastic. The meat was moist, tasted delicious and the feedback was terrific.

His company was founded in March 2010 and set about extending the method to free-range chickens and ducks, marketing them under the Herb-Fed brand.

The life of our Herb-Fed free range chicken (according to Edward Wilkinson):

"A small batch of day-old chickens arrives on the farm each week. They come straight from the hatchery just a few miles up the road and go into a sectioned-off area of our brooding shed where they are kept warm by gas heaters or "brooders" for up to three weeks.

At this stage fresh herbs are introduced into hay racks that are regularly topped up. The herbs are a mixture including basil, chives, dill, coriander and various salads, but their absolute favourite is rocket! The only herb they don't like is sage.

At three weeks they come off the heat as they have developed feathers to keep warm.

Having had a week to get used to the temperature change, our chickens at four weeks old are moved from the brooding shed to a mobile outside shelter where they are truly free range – having constant access to a grass paddock where they use their natural instincts to peck at the grass, find and eat insects, dust bathe and soak up the sunshine.

They are also fed on a locally-produced chicken feed that's a corn-based diet, free from growth promoters and drugs.

Whole corn is mixed in with the feed to give the birds a healthy cover of fat that helps it stay moist once cooked and adds to the flavour of the meat.

By eight weeks the chickens will eat up to a kilogram of fresh herbs each week.

We firmly believe that by feeding our poultry on fresh herbs enhances the natural flavour of the meat giving it a greater depth and an extra dimension.

Furthermore, the herbs give additional nutrients to the chickens' diet and the pecking keeps them occupied – resulting in happy and extremely healthy birds"

HERB-FED TURKEYS

"Our Bronze turkeys arrive with us in June as day-old 'poults' and are carefully nurtured under heat for around six weeks until we feel they are old enough to be allowed into the barn which will become their home.

After a few weeks, the young birds are old enough to be allowed to leave the barn and explore a grass paddock next door. They are now free to come and go from the barn during the day and enjoy foraging in the paddock and feeding on the freshly-cut herbs that supplement their diet.

Each night the birds are locked in the barn where they can enjoy their straw bedding and protection from foxes.

To minimise stress, the turkeys – like the chickens – are slaughtered on site in an approved processing facility.

Birds are dry plucked to give the finest finish and hang for a minimum of 10 days to provide a fuller-flavoured, firmer textured meat."

Turkey – a non-flying bird, originally from America and now intricately connected with Thanksgiving celebrations in the US and Christmas here in the UK.

There are three main varieties, but the white is the most common table bird – for no other reason than the stubble from the plumage is not detectable when plucked and therefore looks cleaner. However some people believe that other breeds – particularly the black and the bronze are gamier and that the whites are too similar in flavour to chicken. The bronze is considered the finest turkey with a good-sized breast but not the massive legs of the white or the black.

Here's my recipe for the perfect roast turkey recipe. You will need:

4.5kg	turkey
100g	butter
2 tsp	sea salt
2 tsp	ground black pepper
½	lemon
½	orange
	thyme leaves
2	bay leaves
12	baby red onions, peeled

The night before roasting, soften the butter and mix with half the salt and pepper.

Remove the giblets from the bird and wipe the inside with kitchen paper. Remove any feathers.

Open the cavity of the bird and season the inside with the remaining salt and pepper. Add the orange, lemon, thyme and bay.

Rub the seasoned butter over the turkey. Cover with greaseproof paper (this will protect the bird while cooking).

Return the turkey to the fridge.

Calculate your cooking times to allow 20 minutes at high heat and then 30 minutes per kilo after that. A 4.5kg bird will therefore take 2.5 hours to cook in total.

Remove the turkey from the fridge about 1-2 hours prior to cooking.

Heat the oven to 220°C.

Place the red onions in the roasting tin and place the turkey on top.

Bring a kettle of water to boil and pour 250ml into the cavity and 500ml into the tray.

Cover the whole thing with tin foil – use two layers and make sure that it is well sealed round the edges.

Place in the oven and cook for 20 minutes then reduce the temperature to 200°C for the remaining cooking time. After approximately 1.5 hours remove the foil and greaseproof paper and place back in the oven – don't open the door again until the cooking time is up.

To test whether the turkey is cooked, insert a skewer or knife into the fattest part of the bird (the breast next to the wings) and the juices should run clear. If still pink, cook for a further 20 minutes and test again.

Allow to rest before carving.

Carving a roast bird

The secret to carving any bird is confidence and a little understanding of how it is put together. You do have to practice, however, so cook a bird every week and in three weeks you will be a master.

Take the bird and, using a long sharp knife, make a cut in between the thigh and the breast. Using the flat of the blade, push the leg away and let the skin tear naturally – the leg should just pop out and you will be left with a good amount of skin still on the breast. Turn the bird around and cut between the wing and the fat end of the breast. Chop these bits any way you like.

Now, once that has been done on both sides of the bird you will be left with what in a professional kitchen is called a crown. Take long thin slices of breast – use a long thin knife and cut with confidence.

Pan-Roast Loin of Round Green Farm Venison with a little Cottage Pie, Roast Garden Vegetables and a Pontefract Cake Sauce

Ingredients

Pan-Roast Loin of Venison

400g	trimmed venison loin
4	sprigs thyme
4	sprigs rosemary
1	clove garlic
20ml	rapeseed oil
4	juniper berries
1 tsp	Womersley apple and geranium jelly

Little Venison Cottage Pie

2	shallots, chopped
½	carrot, chopped
½	stick celery, chopped
½	leek, chopped
20g	mushrooms diced
	sprig of thyme
1	bayleaf
	sprig of rosemary
½ litre	venison stock
400g	venison mince
200ml	red wine
500g	potatoes
30g	butter
20ml	cream
1	egg yolk

Roast Vegetables

300g	parsley root
300g	celeriac
300g	beetroot
300g	butternut squash
300g	parsnip
4	sprigs thyme
4	sprigs rosemary
4	cloves garlic
60ml	rapeseed oil
	salt and pepper
	chopped parsley

Pontefract Cake Sauce

500g	venison bones
30g	carrots
30g	shallots
30g	celery
30g	leek
10g	mushroom
	sprig thyme
	sprig rosemary
	handful of parsley stalks
	bay leaf
4	juniper berries
200ml	red wine
3	Pontefract cakes
20ml	oil for frying

Method

For the Pan-Roast Loin of Venison

Trim all sinew from the venison loin. Tie with string to form a round compact steak.

Lay out a piece of cling film and drizzle with the oil, season with pepper and place the sprigs of rosemary and thyme onto the seasoned cling film with the roast garlic and juniper berries.

Place the venison loin on the cling film and wrap tightly to season and marinade. Leave in the fridge until required.

For the Little Venison Cottage Pie

In a pan brown the venison mince and then remove.

Sweat the vegetables in a pan, then add the browned venison mince, tie the herbs to make a bouquet garni and place into the mince.

Add the red wine and reduce, then add the venison stock.

Peel the potato and boil until soft. Drain and mash. Mix in the cream, butter and egg yolk.

Place into a piping bag with a star nozzle.

When the mince has reduced, season to taste and place in copper pan.

Pipe the creamed potato on top and place in a hot oven to brown the potato.

For the Roast Vegetables

Wash and peel all the vegetables and cut into baton shapes.

Heat a large heavy sauté pan and fry each of the vegetables in the oil until brown. Season with the salt and pepper and toss in the sliced garlic, thyme and rosemary.

Place in a hot oven and roast until soft.

Remove and mix with chopped parsley.

For the Pontefract Cake Sauce

Roast the venison bones and trim until brown.

In a large heavy pan brown the vegetables. Add the herbs and juniper berries.

Deglaze the pan with the red wine, add the browned bones and trim and cover with cold water to cover the bones.

Bring to the boil and skim any scum from the top.

Reduce the heat and simmer for 12 hours.

Pass the stock into a clean pan and reduce until the stock thickens or coats the back of the spoon.

Baked Lamb Faggot in Rich Butter Puff Pastry

(Serves 4)

A different spin on a sausage roll

Ingredients

2	lamb's kidneys
200g	lamb's liver
1	lamb's heart
200g	minced lamb
	pinch chopped rosemary, thyme and parsley
200g	all butter puff pastry
	breadcrumbs
	salt and pepper

Method

In a blender add the prepared kidneys, liver and heart, and pulse until roughly chopped.

Place in a bowl and add the minced lamb, salt, pepper and herbs, and mix together (if the mix is a little wet add a little breadcrumb).

Place the mix into a piping bag.

Roll out the puff pastry and pipe the lamb faggot mix in a line.

Fold over the puff pastry to make a sausage roll shape.

Egg wash and chill.

Cut into 3cm pieces and bake at 180°C until golden brown.

BRAISED FEATHERBLADE OF YORKSHIRE BEEF

(Serves 4)

A real autumn/winter dish this one, great served with creamed potatoes and guaranteed to satisfy the heartiest of appetites.

Ingredients

25g	beef dripping
4	150g featherblade steaks
400g	mirepoix – carrots, onions, leek, celery
1	clove garlic, crushed
1 tsp	tomato purée
125ml	red wine
1 litre	beef stock
1	bouquet garni
	Cornish sea salt and pepper

Method

Season the featherblade steaks on both sides.

Heat the dripping in a hot frying pan and fry the featherblade until golden brown on both sides and place into a braising dish.

In the same pan fry off the mirepoix and garlic until coloured and add the tomato purée and red wine. Reduce by half.

Add the beef stock, bring to the boil and pour over the featherblade.

Place the bouquet garni in the centre of the braising dish. Cover with greaseproof paper and tin foil, then place into the oven at 180°C and cook until tender, approx 1½ hours.

When cooked remove carefully from the braising liquid and keep warm.

Pour the braising liquid into the pan and reduce until you achieve the right consistency.

Check the seasoning and pass through a fine sieve.

Rare Yorkshire Flat Iron Steak

This is the same cut as the featherblade but with all the fat and sinew removed.
Serve this steak medium rare – cooked any longer and it will make the steak tough.

Ingredients

4	200g flat iron steaks
	drizzle of olive oil
	25g butter
	pinch of salt and pepper

Method

Heat a pan until hot, season the flat iron steak with salt and pepper and olive oil.

Place the steaks in the hot pan and leave to seal. After 2 minutes turn the steak over, add the butter and cook for a further 2 minutes.

When cooked, remove from the pan and allow to rest for 5 minutes. Slice and serve.

PAN SEARED RUMP OF LAMB

Simply serve with parsley, mashed potatoes and rosemary gravy. An English dish through and through.

Ingredients

1	rump of lamb, approx 100g
	thyme stalks
	rosemary stalks
1	crushed unpeeled garlic clove
	olive oil
	sea salt and cracked black pepper

Method

The rump of lamb works best if marinated for 12 hours prior to cooking.

Remove the skin of the lamb.

On a sheet of cling film drizzle a little olive oil, sprinkle with salt and pepper, crushed garlic and rosemary.

Place the rump of lamb onto the cling film and tightly wrap. Place in the fridge for 12 hours.

Remove the cling film and in a hot pan drizzle a little olive oil.

Place the lamb rump in a hot pan skin side down and allow to brown evenly.

Carefully turn the rump over, place in the oven at 180°C for 8 minutes and then remove and allow to rest.

Slice and serve.

Pan-Roast Local Pheasant *(Serves 4)* Breast, Smoked Air Dried Bacon, Winter Cabbage and Chestnuts

The longer the birds are hung the stronger the flavours of the meat, we hang ours for three days.

Ingredients

2	whole oven ready pheasants
200g	smoked bacon
½	medium Savoy cabbage
500ml	pheasant or game stock
12	chestnuts, roasted and peeled
4	rashers streaky bacon
25g	butter
75ml	white wine
½	gold rush apple, peeled and diced
125ml	cream
200ml	pheasant or game sauce

Method

Remove the breasts from the pheasants (keep the legs for a terrine).

Wrap each breast with the streaky bacon and set to one side.

Slice the bacon into lardons and in a hot dry pan cook until crispy. Remove and drain off the excess fat and keep to one side.

Shred the cabbage finely and remove any large stalks.

Take a little of the bacon fat and wilt the cabbage in the hot pan and add the apple. Cook a little further then add the white wine and reduce until almost gone and then add the cream and chestnuts and reduce until thick (keep warm).

Season the pheasant breasts and then in a hot pan add a little oil and the butter. Once sizzling add the breasts skin side down and cook on a medium heat for approx 3-4 minutes each side. Be careful not to overcook.

Place the cabbage in the centre of the plate.

Arrange the chestnuts around the cabbage and slice the pheasant breast on top.

Garnish with crispy vegetables.

PLATE OF GREEDY LITTLE PIG

(Serves 6)

Carl's Pigs from Greedy Little Pig are a Gloucestershire Old Spot cross with a Pietrain, the flavour is immense.

Ingredients

For the Pork

1	pork fillet (250g)
1	pork belly (400g)
4 litres	duck fat
4	rashers smoked streaky bacon
5	apples, peeled and cored
50g	butter
100g	sugar
250g	black pudding
4	cheese and chive sausages
2	shallots, finely sliced rings
8	large sage leaves, deep-fried
4	slices Parma ham, dried out

For the Cassoulet

1	carrot
1	onion
1	leek
1	stick celery
100ml	pork stock
100g	haricot beans, soaked and cooked or tinned
250g	chopped tomatoes
	sprig of rosemary
	sprig of thyme
1 tbsp	garlic purée
100g	diced chorizo

Method

For the Pork

Cut the pork fillet into four and wrap each piece in a rasher of bacon. Seal in a hot pan and finish in the oven for 12 minutes.

Cover the pork belly in duck fat, cover with greaseproof and tin foil and cook in the oven for 2½ hours at 150ºC.

Remove from the fat and press with weight until cool. Once cooled and flat, cut into 4 pieces.

Cook sausage and black pudding in the oven for 12 minutes. Crisp the top of the belly pork in a hot pan and warm through with the pork fillet.

For the Cassoulet

Sweat the veg, garlic and chorizo, add chopped tomatoes and haricot beans and 100ml water and bring to boil with the rosemary and thyme. Season to taste and serve alongside the pork.

For the Apple Sauce

Peel and core the apples, sweat down with butter and sugar until soft.

To garnish, flour and deep-fry the shallot rings, deep fry the sage leaves and dry out the Parma ham.

Assemble as the picture and finish with base sauce.

PORK BELLY SLOW-COOKED

(Serves 6)

Ingredients

	pinch of Cornish sea salt
1	stalk lemon grass, chopped roughly
	pinch smoked paprika
	splash of Henderson's Relish
2	cloves garlic, crushed
1kg	pork belly, boned
	drizzle of vegetable oil
	drizzle of sesame seed oil
1 litre	chicken stock

Method

In a pestle and mortar smash the lemon grass, salt, and garlic, then drizzle in the vegetable oil, Henderson's Relish and sesame seed oil to make a paste.

Rub this into the pork belly – all over – and leave to marinade in the fridge for 12-24 hours. The longer you leave the pork belly the stronger the flavour.

Pre-heat the oven to 200°C. Place the marinated pork belly in a roasting tray skin side up and add the chicken stock.

Carefully place the roasting tray onto the stove and bring to the boil.

Cover with greaseproof paper and the double folded tin foil.

Place in a hot oven for 20-30 minutes then turn the oven down to 140°C and cook until tender – approximately 2½ hours.

When cooked allow to cool in the cooking liquor. When cool, remove and slice into 4.

Heat the olive oil in a pan and place the pork skin side down for 10 minutes to crackle up the skin. Then turn over and place in the oven to warm through for 10 minutes.

PRESSED GREEDY LITTLE PIG

Ingredients

3	ham knuckles
	mirepoix of carrot, onion, leek, celery and garlic
	bouquet garni of bay leaf, thyme, sage stalks
	pinch black peppercorns
8	cloves
	small bunch flat leaf parsley
1 tbsp	whole grain mustard
2	sheets gelatine
2	banana shallots, finely chopped
	ground black pepper
8	slices York ham or Parma ham

Pressed Greedy Little Pig Garnish

8	asparagus, peeled and trimmed
100g	peas, blanched and shelled
100g	broad beans, shelled
1	shallot, diced
	half a galia melon
	pickling juice (See Mackerel recipe)
	mustard dressing
100ml	ham stock
	bunch of watercress
100g	frozen peas
100g	broad beans
25g	butter

Method

Place the ham knuckles, mirepoix and bouquet garni tied with string, cloves and peppercorns in a large pan and cover with cold water. Bring to the boil, skim and then simmer for 2½-3 hours until tender.

Keep topping up the pan so that the hocks are always covered.

Line the terrine mould with cling film and then with the ham.

Once the hams are cooked (you can tell this as the small bone in the knuckle will remove easily from the meat) remove from the pan and leave to cool slightly as they are just too hot to handle. Then, while warm remove the meat from the bone.

Place in a bowl with the shallots, seasoning and parsley. Mix and combine thoroughly, then pack into the terrine mould.

Ladle 500ml of the ham hock stock into a pan. Warm gently before adding the gelatine and pour the liquid over the ham terrine. Fold over the ham to cover the ham pieces and cover with cling film.

Place a weight on top – some tins from your cupboard will do – and leave overnight in the fridge.

Turn out the terrine, unwrap and with a sharp knife, slice the terrine about a finger thick.

For the Melon

Peel, deseed and dice into squares, pour over warm pickling juice.

For the Pea Purée

Heat the butter over a medium heat and add the shallot and cook until soft, but not coloured, about 1-2 minutes.

Add the ham stock and bring to the boil.

Add the peas and cook for 1-2 minutes. Remove from the heat.

Add the watercress and then blend in a food processor until smooth. Pass through a fine sieve.

Correct the seasoning.

To serve

Blanch the asparagus, peas and broad beans and refresh. Drain and place in a small bowl.

Mix in the diced shallots, season with salt and pepper and toss through 1 tablespoon of mustard dressing.

To finish the dish, place a spoon of pea and watercress purée on the plate and smudge.

Slice and add the greedy little pig terrine.

Dress on top of the terrine with the asparagus pea and broad bean mix and garnish with the melon, baby watercress and a drizzle of olive oil.

ROAST MILK-FED SUCKLING PIG

Ingredients

For the Suckling Pig

3.4-5kg	suckling pig, boned out (head and trotters on)
2.5kg	rolled medallions of pork, skin removed
	pig trivet
2	carrots
1	leek
2	sticks celery
½	bulb garlic
6	shallots
500g	apple and Calvados stuffing (See recipe below)

For the Apple and Calvados Stuffing

250g	dried apple
250g	pork, trimmed and chopped
1	orange zest
100g	fresh breadcrumbs
100ml	Calvados
150ml	Ampleforth cider
	small bunch sage chopped
	sea salt and ground black pepper
	grated nutmeg

Method

Place the boned baby pig on the bench, skin side down so that the cavity is open, and season with salt and pepper.

Spread the inside of the baby pig with the apple stuffing.

Place the medallions of pork into the cavity of the baby pig.

Sew up the cavity with twine using an upholstery needle, threading the twine about 2cm apart on both sides of the belly (making sure that you do not overlap the belly as it would not crackle up).

Place the pig (trivet) vegetables on to a tray large enough to fit the piglet and place the piglet on it (sphinx like) e.g. belly down with its legs on the side of the body.

Rub the whole piglet with a good helping of olive oil and cover the ears and tail in foil (to prevent them from burning).

Season with sea salt.

Place into an oven at 180ºC and roast for 2½-3 hours.

Remove from the oven and allow to rest for 30 minutes.

The pig skin should be crisp and the meat moist.

Carefully remove the roasted piglet and set on a serving platter.

Strain the cooking juice, skim off the fat and boil the pig juices.

Add a little of the pork stock and season.

For the Apple and Calvados Stuffing

Roughly chop the apples.

Add the chopped pork, sage, breadcrumbs, Calvados, cider, zest and chopped sage. Season with salt and pepper and a little grated nutmeg to form the stuffing.

Roast Bone Marrow With Toasted Brioche, Caper, Parsley and Watercress Salad

(Serves 4)

I can always remember as a child at my nana's sucking the marrow bone from the Sunday roast leg of lamb. Fergus Henderson is notorious for serving them at his restaurant, St John's in London.

Ingredients

12	6cm pieces of veal marrow bone
	Cornish sea salt and cracked black pepper
	sprig thyme
1	bay leaf
	small bunch of flat leaf parsley
2 tbsp	finely sliced capers
2	shallots, peeled and sliced finely into rings
	handful of watercress
1	lemon
	basic salad dressing

Method

Heat the oven to 180°C. Season both ends of the marrow bone with salt and pepper. Place in a roasting tray with the thyme and bay leaf. Place in the oven and roast for about 20 minutes.

The marrow bone should be soft, if not, roast for longer until it melts into an oily mess.

Place the watercress, shallots, capers and parsley into a bowl and dress with a tablespoon of basic salad dressing and a squeeze of lemon juice.

Toast the brioche and serve the marrow bone standing up on the brioche and dressed watercress salad.

BRAISED NECK OF LAMB   (Serves 4)

Slow-cooked with a great flavour.

Ingredients

For the Braised Neck

4	lamb necks cut through the bone (ask your butcher to do this)
60g	dripping

For the Mirepoix of Vegetables

100g	chopped shallot
100g	chopped celery
100g	chopped carrot
100g	chopped leek
2	cloves garlic, chopped

For the Bouquet Garni

thyme, bay, rosemary and parsley stalks tied together with string

250ml	red wine
60g	tomato purée
175g	chopped fresh or tinned tomatoes

2 litres fresh lamb stock

Method

Heat a thick bottomed frying pan (make sure that it can go into the oven).

Season the lamb neck with salt and pepper.

Add the dripping to the pan and fry the lamb neck on both sides until golden brown.

Remove from the pan and set aside. Add the mirepoix of vegetables and cook for 3 minutes then add the chopped garlic and bouquet garni and cook for a further 3-4 minutes.

Stir in the tomato purée and cook this for 3 minutes.

Add the chopped tomatoes then add the red wine and reduce by two thirds.

Season with a little more salt and pepper (don't over season as the liquor will become stronger later in the cooking process).

Place the lamb neck back in the pan and cover with the lamb stock.

Bring slowly to the boil, skim and cover with greaseproof paper and a tight fitting lid (double folded tin foil works as well).

Place in a moderate oven 180°C and cook for 1½ hours or until the neck meat is tender.

When cooked and tender remove the lamb necks from the sauce and keep warm.

Place the sauce back onto the stove and reduce. Remove any fat and adjust the consistency and seasoning.

Pass the sauce through a fine strainer and serve over the lamb neck.

Slow-Cooked Marinated Breast of Lamb

Ingredients

1	breast of lamb, boned
2	cloves garlic, chopped
	rosemary, finely chopped
	thyme leaves, picked
	olive oil

Method

Lay the breast of lamb out flat with the skin side down. Remove the breast bones (roast and use for stock).

Rub the chopped garlic into the lamb breast. Sprinkle on the thyme and rosemary and season with salt and pepper.

Roll the lamb breast up tightly and wrap in cling film and then wrap in double foil.

Place in the fridge and leave for 12 hours.

Remove from the fridge and place in a roasting tray and half cover with boiling water. Place into the oven at 150°C and cook for 2-2½ hours.

When cooked remove the foil and cling film and slice.

We serve this fried in a little butter to crisp up the belly – the contrast in texture makes all the difference.

GAME TERRINE

Use whatever game you can get for this tasty recipe. It requires a little work, but the results are well worth the effort.

Ingredients

Selection of lean game meat, about 1kg in all, which could include:

> breasts of pheasant (hung about 5 days)
>
> breasts of pigeon
>
> breasts of duck or other wild fowl
>
> saddle and hindquarters of rabbit, boned
>
> saddle and hindquarters of hare, boned
>
> lean strips of venison (from the leg or fillet)
>
> oil or fat, for frying

For the forcemeat:

500g	sausage meat
	livers from all the game, finely chopped
2	handfuls fresh white breadcrumbs
1	egg
3 tbsp	parsley, finely chopped
	few sprigs of thyme, leaves removed and chopped
5-6	juniper berries, crushed in pestle and mortar
2	cloves garlic, finely chopped
	splash of brandy
	splash of red wine
	salt and pepper

To line the dish:

300g	streaky bacon, flattened with the back of a knife

Method

In a large mixing bowl combine the sausage meat and the chopped livers from the game.

Next add the breadcrumbs, egg, parsley, thyme, juniper berries and garlic. Then add the wine and brandy, season with the salt and pepper and mix everything together thoroughly, preferably with your hands.

Cut the game meat into roughly same-size strips, about 2 fingers thick.

In a heavy-based frying pan heat the fat or oil and fry the game pieces for 2 minutes until nicely browned.

Line a loaf tin or ceramic terrine dish with the stretched rashers of streaky bacon. Add a layer of forcemeat followed by a layer of game meat, then a layer of forcemeat followed by another layer of game meat. (If you like, you can put the same kind of meat in each layer, i.e. a layer of rabbit, a layer of pigeon and then a layer of pheasant). However many layers you make (I usually go for 3) be sure to finish with a layer of the forcemeat.

Fold the exposed strips of bacon over the top of the terrine and cover well with kitchen foil. If your terrine dish has a lid on it, so much the better.

Place the terrine dish in a roasting tin half-filled with hot water. Cook in the oven at 160°C for approximately 1½-2 hours.

Test with a skewer to see if it is cooked. If the skewer does not come out of the terrine piping hot, then it is not ready.

For the best possible texture and easy slicing, your terrine should be pressed as it cools. Find a piece of wood or plastic that fits snugly inside the terrine dish and weigh it down with a brick or 2. (Another similar size dish or loaf tin with a brick inside often does the trick, but wrap it in cling film if you're using a tin.)

Leave the terrine until completely cold for several hours or overnight.

To serve the terrine

Slice it thickly with a very sharp knife, put on a plate with a small salad of lightly dressed green leaves and a blob of good fruit chutney. Serve with hot toast.

Yorkshire
Piccalilli

Built on quality and

Roast Rack of Spring Lamb with Provençale Crumb and Roast Spring Vegetables

(Serves 4)

Ingredients

4	racks of 4-bone lamb chined and French trimmed
10g	Dijon mustard
100g	Provençale bread crumbs (See basic recipes)
4	large shallots peeled cut in half and roasted
8	spears English asparagus trimmed
100g	Heritage carrots yellow, washed trimmed and blanched
100g	Heritage carrots white, washed trimmed and blanched
100g	Heritage carrots purple, washed trimmed and blanched
6	medium Jersey potatoes, cooked
100g	baby leaf spinach, washed
	salt and pepper
200ml	lamb stock
	sprig rosemary
	drizzle of pesto (See basic recipes)

Method

Preheat the oven to 240°C.

Prepare the herb crust.

Heat the oil in a large pan with the butter until foaming but not coloured.

Season the racks and add to the pan, skin-side down, and cook for 3-4 minutes on each side (for medium rare). Remove from the pan and leave to rest for 5 minutes.

Place the racks of lamb, fat side up, on a chopping board and brush the mustard over the racks to apply a good coating.

Press a generous handful of the herb crust over the racks and transfer to a medium-sized roasting tin and roast for 5-15 minutes, depending on how your lamb is preferred. Cover the bones with foil if browning too quickly.

To make the jus, heat the stock and rosemary in a pan over a medium to high heat and reduce by half, stirring occasionally. Check seasoning, strain and keep warm.

In a clean sauté pan over a medium heat add the cooked potatoes and colour slightly.

Add the carrots and asparagus and toss with the potatoes and place in the oven.

When soft remove from the oven and toss in the spinach to wilt. Season with salt and pepper.

Slice the racks in half and serve immediately with the roasted spring vegetables – and a drizzle of basil pesto.

ROAST PORK HOCK
WITH RHUBARB

(Serves 4)

Ingredients

4	ham hocks, washed in cold water for 2 hours
4	large shallots
6	cloves garlic
5cm	fresh ginger, peeled and grated
3 tbsp	honey
2 tbsp	whole grain mustard
	pinch of ground black pepper
	glug of olive oil
½ pint	cider
500g	rhubarb
250g	Bramley apples

Method

Boil the ham hocks for 2½ hours (or until the small bone removes easy) with the shallots, cloves garlic and ginger. When cooked remove from the liquid and allow to cool slightly.

Remove the outer skin and fat. Remove the small bone by slightly twisting and pulling. (You will know when the ham hocks are cooked as this bone will remove easily and cleanly).

In a bowl, mix the honey, pepper and mustard together.

Place the ham hocks in the bowl and rub the honey mixture into them.

In a roasting tray, place the chopped rhubarb and apples, add a glug of olive oil and add the cider.

Place the ham hocks on top and roast in the oven at 200°C for 20 minutes or until the ham hocks are slightly caught on the outside and the apple and rhubarb are soft.

Remove the hocks and stir the apple and rhubarb. Place the hocks on a plate and spoon over the rhubarb.

This is a great dinner party dish as you could serve it straight from the oven.

Yorkshire Puddings with Lamb Faggots and Yorkshire Ale Gravy

(Serves 4)

This is a great little dish and I can still remember my nana making these for me and my granddad, Oliver, in Knottingley, on a lunchtime when I would go round to have my school lunch.

Ingredients

8 or 12	Yorkshire puddings
150g	lamb's liver
150g	lamb's kidney
100g	lamb's heart
100g	pig's caul fat
100g	breadcrumbs
400ml	brown stock
¼ pint	real Yorkshire ale

Method

For the faggots, first mince or chop the liver, kidneys and heart until quite coarse and place in a bowl. Season with a little salt and pepper and some thyme leaves and finely chopped rosemary. Mix with a spoon.

If the liver mixture is a little wet, add some breadcrumbs just to stiffen the mixture.

Lay out the pig's caul and pat dry with kitchen paper.

With a dessertspoon, shape the mixture into 8 ball shapes and cut a piece of pig's caul large enough to wrap around each one. Wrap securely and overlap slightly.

To cook, heat a non-stick pan, add a little rapeseed oil and knob of butter and place the faggots smooth side down and cook for 1 minute. Turn the faggots and cook for a further minute. Baste the faggots, add a little more butter if required, and place into a moderate oven approximately 180°C for 10 minutes.

Remove the faggots and allow to rest.

Remove the fat from the pan and place the pan back on a low heat. Add the ale, stirring the bottom of the pan and lifting all those nice bits off the bottom, and let the ale reduce by half.

Add the stock and bring to the boil and season with salt and pepper.

Place the faggots into the Yorkshire puddings and the ale gravy.

Garnish with a little sprig of thyme and serve.

PUDDINGS
and Sweet Things

The one thing I've learned as a professional chef is that the pastry section is one of the most demanding, time-consuming and yet satisfying areas of the kitchen.

Chefs generally start work at the same time, but the pastry chef is always the last to leave.

He or she has to follow the recipes to the letter, unlike colleagues elsewhere who have the luxury of substituting a certain ingredient if they don't happen to have it. Desserts are more of a science. Sugars, flours and eggs all work together like a mathematical equation and if you follow the recipes step by step, the result will be something to be proud of time and time again.

SWEET PASTE

Ingredients

250g	plain flour
100g	icing sugar
140g	butter
1	egg
	pinch salt

Method

Sieve the flour and salt into a bowl. Lightly rub in the butter until a sandy texture is achieved.

In a separate bowl, beat the egg and icing sugar.

Make a well in the centre and pour in the egg and sugar mix.

Gradually mix in the flour to form a smooth paste.

Make sure that you do not overwork the paste as this will toughen the finished result.

YUMMY YORKSHIRE
Ice Cream

We had only been open a month or so and my time in the kitchen was stretched to the limit. But Jeremy and Louise Holmes, of Yummy Yorkshire, were dining with a group of friends and asked to see me.

"Who makes your ice cream?" I was asked. "I do. I have a two litre ice cream machine in the pastry section and start making ice cream from 7am and finish at around 10pm. Why?"

"Well, we make ice cream. Why don't you come up and try some?"

A week or two later I took them up on their offer and went with my son Henry to their ice cream parlour. I was totally blown away by Louise's ice cream and some of their unusual flavours.

Now all my ice cream comes from Jeremy and Louise and we have become very good friends.

ROBERT...
and his Rhubarb

Robert Tomlinson knows a bit about rhubarb. And so he should. After all, it's been the family business for four generations.

He can trace the connection all the way back to his great-grandad's aunt, who started the company back in 1880. In those days they were based in Pudsey, West Yorkshire, on 85 acres of land. The years since then have seen wildly fluctuating fortunes. In the early 1970s Tomlinsons had 12 rhubarb sheds. Today there are three. Even so, the outlook now is much brighter than the days when rhubarb was out of fashion and the business operated from just one.

Before the Second World War there were 200 growers in Yorkshire. In the night hours, tons of the stuff would be loaded onto the express train from Leeds to London. Those heady days are now only a memory, and there remain eleven growers in what is known as the Rhubarb Triangle, drawn on a line linking Leeds, Bradford and Wakefield. This traditional way of growing rhubarb now commands Protected Designation of Origin status. The PDO is there to protect the name and uniqueness of Yorkshire rhubarb from the deluge of foreign imports such as those from Holland which imitate the forcing method. It also serves to reassure the customer when buying Yorkshire forced rhubarb that it is of the expected flavour and quality, and grown in the traditional manner.

B. TOMLINSON &
MOSS HOUSE FARM • ROKER
PUDSEY • WEST YORKSHIRE • LS
TEL: 0113 256 5832 & 0113 256 9027 • MOB: 07

Rhubarb

This all starts with 2-year-old rhubarb roots that have been planted outside. These are left to grow and then die back so all the nutrients go back into the root. This is repeated for two years. After exposure to the harsh frost the plants are then lifted and planted in the rhubarb sheds. Here they are deprived of light and food which 'forces' the root to begin to grow. This happens quickly and when all is quiet you can hear a 'pop' as the stalk pushes itself out of the budded sheaf.

It's often possible to see candles glowing in the rhubarb sheds. This is so the picker can see to work. The rhubarb itself is shielded from any light, as this would stop the growing process. All the forced rhubarb is laid and picked by hand – back-breaking work at the best of times, but Robert's dad is quick to remind us that the shed used to be a lot lower in his day. Each stem must be removed intact from the roots as anything that's left can cause rotting.

There are over 100 varieties of rhubarb today, here are just three that merit the accolade of Bilton's best;

Stocksbridge Arrow

Raspberry Red

Timpelly Old Variety (good outside grower)

ASSIETTE OF RHUBARB *(Serves 6)*

Ingredients

Rhubarb Crumble

For the filling

900g	rhubarb, topped and tailed
50g	butter
1	orange, juice and zest
1	lemon, juice only

For the topping

100g	butter, diced and cold
150g	plain flour
50g	oatflakes
80g	soft brown sugar

Rhubarb Jelly

½ pt	water
100g	caster sugar
2	rhubarb stems, washed and chopped
8	gelatine leaves

Rhubarb Pannacotta

¼ pt	milk
80g	mascarpone cheese
1	vanilla pod, split
1	gelatine leaf

Method

To prepare the filling, peel, core and chop the apples.

Place in a large saucepan with the butter and cook slowly on a low heat until tender (approx 10 minutes).

Add the gooseberries and cook for a further 5 minutes.

Add the sugar, lemon and orange zest.

Taste for sweetness and add a little more sugar if required as the gooseberries can be quite sharp.

For the topping, sift the flour into a bowl and rub in the diced cold butter.

The mixture should look like breadcrumbs.

Fold in the sugar and oatflakes.

Boil the water and sugar and then add the chopped rhubarb.

Once the mixture is soft, sieve over a bowl to retain the juice and reserve the rhubarb for the pannacotta.

Soak the gelatine in cold water until soft. Squeeze dry and add to the rhubarb water. Pour into shot glasses and allow to set.

Boil the milk with the split vanilla pod, stirring to disperse the seeds through the milk.

Once boiling, remove from heat.

Soak the gelatine in cold water and when soft squeeze dry.

Add to the milk and mix through until melted. Remove the vanilla pod.

Whisk in the mascarpone cheese and allow to cool.

Place some rhubarb compote from the jelly into shot glasses and top with the pannacotta mix.

Allow to set.

RICE PUDDING

(Serves 6)

Rice pudding is amazingly versatile. Just before the rice is cooked, add 100g of blackberries to the rice for a fantastic flavour and colour. Or a good dollop of raspberry jam or lemon curd goes perfectly with the dish, as does a drizzle of local honey. I prefer my rice pudding served cold. When cooled, just fold in 100ml whipped cream.

Ingredients

500ml	cream
200ml	milk
1	vanilla pod, split in half, seeds scraped out
90g	pudding rice (you can also use risotto rice or any short grain rice)
50g	butter (optional)
75g	caster sugar
	freshly grated nutmeg

Method

Wash the pudding rice in running cold water.

In a heavy-based pan, heat the cream, milk, butter, vanilla and sugar.

When the cream and milk are coming to the boil, add the washed rice and bring to the boil, stirring continuously.

Reduce the heat to very low and continue to stir frequently.

By the time the rice is cooked, the cream and milk should be thick and coating the rice.

Remove the vanilla pod (this can be washed and added to a jar of sugar to make vanilla sugar for baking).

Ladle into dishes, grate on a little nutmeg and serve.

CHOCOLATE MARQUISE

(Serves 8)

'I'd give up chocolate but I'm no quitter'. I know what you mean.

Ingredients

250g	melted dark chocolate
12	egg yolks
250g	caster sugar
3 tbsp	instant coffee
60ml	boiling water
100g	honey
275g	butter
165g	cocoa powder
450ml	cream

Method

Mix the egg yolks, dissolved coffee and sugar over a bain marie until thick. Add the melted chocolate and honey. Mix well.

Cream the butter and then add the cocoa powder.

Add the butter mixture to the egg mixture.

Whip the cream to soft peaks and fold into the chocolate mix.

Place in moulds and leave to chill for 24 hours.

CHOCOLATE TART

(Serves 8)

Ingredients

380g	dark chocolate (70%)
250g	unsalted butter
4	eggs
6	egg yolks
70g	caster sugar
1	pre-baked tart shell

Method

Place the chocolate in a bowl and melt over a bain marie – stir occasionally, until smooth. Cool.

Pre-heat oven to 150ºC.

Whisk eggs and the egg yolks with the sugar until thick and pale. Carefully fold into the chocolate mixture and pour into the pre-baked tart shell.

Bake for approximately 12-15 minutes.

Remove from the oven and allow to rest for 1 hour.

WHITE CHOCOLATE CRÈME BRÛLEÉ

Simply add a little grated orange zest to the cream and taste the difference

Ingredients

7	egg yolks
1	pint cream
100g	white chocolate
75g	caster sugar
1	vanilla pod, split
	extra caster sugar for sprinkling

Method

Pre-heat the oven to 150°C.

In a heavy-bottomed pan slowly bring the cream, vanilla pod and half the sugar to just boiling point.

Whisk the egg yolks and the remaining sugar together until the mixture is pale and thick. At this stage add the chocolate to the milk and stir until melted.

Pour over the egg mix, giving it a light stir with the whisk. Transfer the mixture into a jug and carefully pour into ramekins or dishes.

Place these in a tray of hot water deep enough to come halfway up the dishes. Place in the oven and cook slowly until the crème brulee has set (approximately 10 minutes).

Remove from the oven, take out the brulees and allow to cool.

Just before serving, sprinkle with caster sugar. Using a blow torch, caramelise the top.

Allow to cool slightly and serve.

CLASSIC LEMON TART

(Serves 16)

To make it easier, pour half the mixture in the flan case and then place into the oven. Then pour the rest of the mix into the tart while on the rack in the oven. This will stop any spillage over the sides.

Ingredients

1	lined flan ring of sugar paste, blind baked
12	eggs
3	egg yolks
400g	caster sugar
450ml	cream
	juice of 6 lemons, zest of 3

Method

Pre-heat the oven to 180°C.

Whisk the zest, sugar and eggs together. Mix in the lemon juice.

In a pan, bring the cream almost to the boil, then mix into the lemon and egg mix.

Remove the froth from the top.

Reduce the oven temperature to 120°C and pour the lemon tart mix into the flan case. Carefully place into the oven. Cook for 30 minutes or until the lemon tart is just set.

Allow to cool slightly before removing from the ring.

Slice into 16, dredge each slice with icing sugar and blow torch until the top has a nice sugar caramel top.

Gooseberry, Apple and Victoria Plum Crumble

(Serves 8)

Ingredients

For the filling

250g	gooseberries, top and tailed
250g	Victoria plums, stoned
500g	Bramley apples
50g	butter
	juice and zest of 1 orange
	juice of 1 lemon

For the topping

100g	butter, diced and chilled in the fridge
150g	plain flour
50g	oat flakes
80g	soft brown sugar

Method

For the filling

Peel, core and chop the apples. Place into a large saucepan with the butter and cook slowly on a low heat until tender – approximately 10 minutes.

Add the gooseberries and plums then cook for a further 5 minutes.

Stir in the sugar, lemon and orange zest.

Taste for sweetness and add a little more sugar if required.

For the topping

Sift the flour into a bowl and rub in the diced cold butter. The mixture should look like breadcrumbs. Fold in the sugar and oat flakes.

To serve

Add the filling to individual ramekins and top with a generous spoonful of the crumble mixture.

Bake in a moderately hot oven 160°C, for around 10 minutes, or until the topping is golden brown.

Serve with Crème Anglaise.

SHARROW BAY STICKY TOFFEE PUDDING

(Serves 6)

Now a commonplace item on menus everywhere, this recipe comes from the legendary Sharrow Bay Hotel in Windermere and a great chef in Francis Coulson.

Ingredients

100g	butter
300g	caster sugar
2	eggs
300g	chopped dates
2 tsp	bicarbonate of soda
1 pint	boiling water
400g	self-raising flour
2 tsp	baking powder

Method

Place the chopped dates and bicarbonate of soda in a bowl and cover with the boiling water.

Cream the butter and sugar until light and fluffy.

Add the eggs one at a time.

Sift the flour and baking powder and add to the butter mix.

Combine the date mixture.

Allow to rest.

Place into moulds and cook at 160ºC for 15–20 minutes.

CRÈME ANGLAISE

Leave the vanilla pod in the anglaise to intensify the flavour.

Ingredients

¼ litre	milk
¼ litre	cream
1	vanilla pod, split
4	egg yolks
300g	sugar

Method

Boil the milk, cream, vanilla and half the sugar. Remove and cool.

Whisk the egg yolks and the remaining sugar until pale over a bain marie.

Add milk to egg mix and return to heat – do not re-boil.

Place in cold bowl.

LEMON POSSET

(Serves 4)

This is a dish with a bit of zing that has been pleasing people for centuries. Serve with fresh raspberries to add another flavour dimension.

Ingredients

400ml	cream
125g	caster sugar
1½	lemons, zest and juice

Method

Boil the cream and sugar, then stir in the lemon juice and zest. Allow to cool.

Place into glasses.

THE YORKSHIRE PUDDING 'PUDDING'

(Serves 6)

Best served warm and with a dollop of raspberry ripple ice cream.
This is my version of that old classic bread and butter pudding and the French croissant butter pudding. But being a true Yorkshireman I don't like to waste anything. So after Sunday lunch any spare Yorkshire puddings are put to good use as part of a dessert course.
The trick here is not to overcook the pudding – and to eat it while still warm.

Ingredients

250ml	milk
250ml	whipping cream
1	vanilla pod, split
4	whole eggs
2	egg yolks
150g	caster sugar
6-8	large Yorkshire puddings (See basic recipes)
25g	yellow sultanas
25g	melted butter
125g	shaved white chocolate
	shot of whisky or brandy
	raspberry jam
	icing sugar for dusting

Method

Boil the milk and cream with the vanilla pod.

Remove the pod and crumble in the white chocolate. Remove from the heat and stir until the chocolate is melted.

In a separate bowl, whisk the eggs and egg yolks with the caster sugar. Put the milk and cream mixture into the egg mix and whisk again.

Pour over the Yorkshires and sultanas and bake in the oven for 20-25 minutes or until almost set.

Remove from the oven and sprinkle with icing sugar.

Caramelise under the grill or use a blow torch.

Remove from the grill and brush with hot raspberry jam.

BREAD AND BUTTER PUDDING

Here we have added marmalade to this old favourite. Don't over-fill your dish with the bread; make sure there is plenty of the egg and milk mix to make the pudding feel nice and light.

Ingredients

30g	sultanas
6	slices of bread
4	eggs
1 pint	milk
½	vanilla pod with seeds
35cl	Grand Marnier
30g	sugar (save 10g to sprinkle on top)
1 tbsp	marmalade
1	zest of an orange

Method

Place the sultanas, sugar and brandy in a bowl. Mix and leave to stand for approximately 2 hours.

Butter the bread and dish.

Remove the crusts from the bread and cut into triangles.

Heat the milk with the vanilla pod, seeds and sugar to just boiling.

In a separate bowl, whisk the eggs.

When the milk is just at boiling point strain over the eggs and combine thoroughly.

Neatly lay the buttered bread in the dish and sprinkle with the marinated sultanas.

Repeat the process in the opposite direction to create another layer.

When the final layer is complete, pour over the hot egg custard mix.

Sprinkle with sugar and cook in a bain-marie (bath of hot water) at 160ºC for 20 minutes or until the egg mixture is set.

In a small pan heat the apricot jam with a drop of water and brush over the cooked bread and butter pudding.

THE KNIVES
Are Out...

Just make sure you get the right one.

Now you might have looked at my trademark TB logo and got the idea I have a thing about knives. And it's true, I do. But not in the way you might think.

Granted, I have my initials spelled out in the things.

There is a reason for that. I wanted to reinforce the fact that we're working chefs here, using the same tools of the trade chefs have used for centuries. If others want to be represented by a microwave or boil-in-the-bag creations, that's their lookout. The knife is the basic starting point from which preparation of fresh food starts. There is labour involved, and skill in addition.

Of all the tools in the cook's armoury, a proper set of knives is easily the most important. Contrary to popular belief, there isn't one brand that's particularly favoured in professional kitchens. Most of the best-known European and Far-Eastern manufacturers produce knives that are up to the task, certainly the kind of use they're likely to get in the kitchen of a typical home. When you buy yours, pick some from the shelves and grip them firmly. The right knife should feel comfortable to grip. It should be an extension of your hand.

The crucial thing to remember is that your knives should be kept sharp. I've seen, all too often, chefs cut themselves. It's an occupational hazard. But I've also seen far more of them injured with a blunt knife rather than a sharp one. With a blunt knife, more pressure is required when cutting. So should your hand slip, the consequence will be worse because you're pressing harder.

Stay sharp. Stay safe.

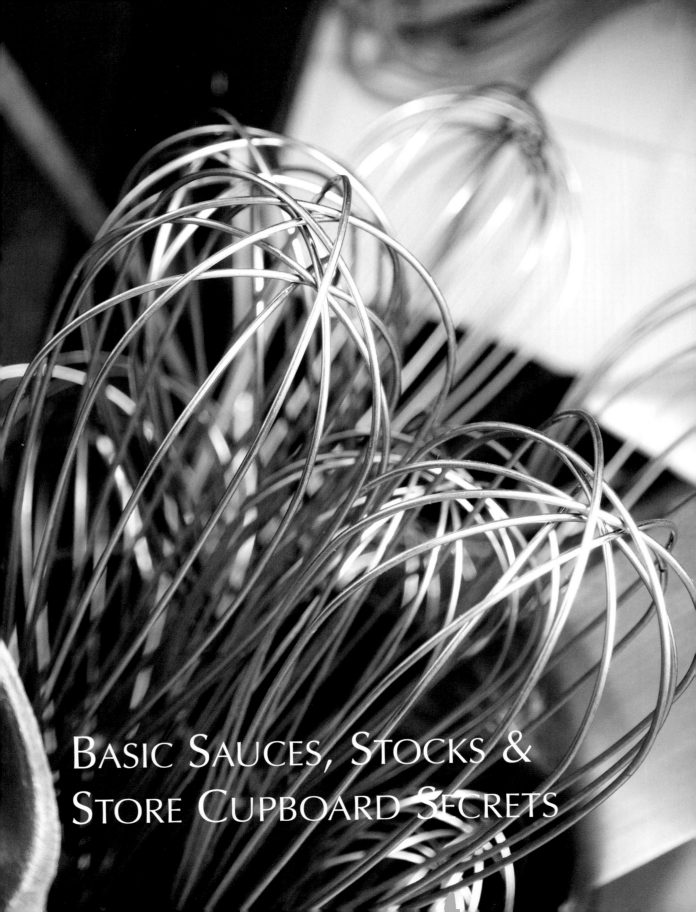

BASIC SAUCES, STOCKS &
STORE CUPBOARD SECRETS

PROVENÇALE BREADCRUMBS

This herb crumb is great with lamb and fish.

Ingredients

2	slices bread
½	clove garlic, puréed
5g	flat leaf parsley
1 tsp	thyme leaves
1 tsp	finely chopped rosemary
½	zest orange
½	zest lemon
2 tbsp	extra virgin olive oil
	pinch salt
	fresh milled pepper

Method

In a robot coupe, place the bread, parsley, thyme, rosemary, salt and pepper, and blitz until you have breadcrumbs. The bread will take on the green colour from the parsley.

Remove and place in a bowl add the zest of the orange and lemon, and drizzle in the olive oil.

Check the seasoning.

CHASSEUR SAUCE

This classic sauce is best served with a juicy steak or plump chicken breast.

Ingredients

25g	butter
125g	button mushrooms, sliced
25g	diced shallots
½	clove garlic
125g	tomatoes, peeled, seeded and chopped
25g	tomato purée
125ml	red wine
250ml	reduced beef or veal stock
1 tbsp	chopped tarragon
	pinch of salt and pepper
	bouquet garni

Method

Melt the butter in a pan and sweat the shallots, add the garlic and bouquet garni.

Place the sliced mushrooms in the pan and cook for a further 3 minutes. Add tomato purée and cook for a further minute then add the red wine and reduce by half.

Place in the stock and slowly bring to the boil, skim the top of the sauce.

Add the tomato concasse and chopped tarragon.

Check for seasoning and serve.

CHIMICHURRI

"Jimmy who?" My young son looked perplexed, clearly hoping I was bringing news of a South American star about to sign for Leeds. No such luck. We're talking about an Argentine parsley and garlic sauce for grilled meat. This pungent herb sauce originated in Argentina. Chimichurri is the classic accompaniment to Argentine Churassco, or grilled meats. Chimichurri is also used as a marinade.

Ingredients

1	bunch of flat leaf parsley, chopped
8	cloves garlic, crushed
	pinch oregano
1 tbsp	paprika
½ tsp	cayenne pepper
	pinch salt
1	zest and juice of lime
200ml	red wine vinegar
600ml	olive oil

Method

Put the parsley, garlic, oregano, paprika, salt, cayenne, zest and juice of the lime and vinegar into a blender and pulse to process well. Do not purée – leave a little chunky.

Remove and stir in the olive oil.

Let it stand for at least 30 minutes for the flavours to marry together.

Serve at room temperature.

PESTO

Great tossed through some pasta.

Ingredients

	big handful basil
	handful parsley (Italian flat leaf)
20g	Parmesan cheese, finely grated
10g	pine kernels
500ml	olive oil
	pinch salt and pepper

Variations can be made from:

rocket

wild garlic

Method

Pick the leaves from the basil stalks/parsley. Wash and place in a food processor.

Add the Parmesan, pine nuts, salt and pepper and a glug of olive oil.

Blitz in the food processor and gradually add the rest of the olive oil to give the pesto a creamy texture.

Correct the seasoning.

This will keep in an airtight container for up to two weeks.

BEURRE BLANC

Ingredients

40g	shallots, finely sliced
1 tbsp	white wine vinegar
3 tbsp	white wine
3 tbsp	cream
250g	unsalted butter, diced and chilled
	lemon juice
	salt and pepper

Method

In a pan, fry the shallots with a little butter until soft.

Add the vinegar and white wine. Reduce by half.

Add the cream and bring to the boil.

Remove from the heat and whisk in the butter.

Season with salt, pepper and lemon juice.

Variations:

Scent the beurre blanc with: tarragon, basil, coriander, thyme, rosemary, cucumber, cardamom or ginger.

CUMBERLAND SAUCE

Great served with cold game meat.

Ingredients

250g	redcurrant jelly
125ml	port
25g	shallots, finely chopped
½	lemon zest and juice
1	orange zest and juice
1 tsp	English mustard
	dusting of ground ginger (optional)
	drizzle olive oil

Method

Warm the olive oil in a pan and sweat the shallots.

Add the port, mustard, lemon and orange zest and juice and ginger.

Bring slowly to the boil to allow the redcurrant jelly to melt.

Allow to cool and serve.

OUR SALAD DRESSING

Ingredients

1 tsp	Dijon mustard
1 tbsp	white wine vinegar
4 tbsp	olive oil
	pinch of salt and pepper

Method

Place the Dijon mustard and white wine vinegar into a bowl and whisk.

Add the salt and pepper (this is to dissolve the salt).

If you add it after the oil the dressing will be gritty.

Whisk in the olive oil and store in the fridge.

GARDEN HERB DRESSING

Ingredients

	large bunch parsley, flat leaf
	chives
1	clove garlic
	pinch pinenuts
25g	Parmesan cheese
175ml	rapeseed oil

Method

Place all the ingredients in a bowl and with a hand blender blitz everything together.

Season with salt and pepper.

APPLE SAUCE

(Makes about 275ml)

Ingredients

500g	Bramley apples
½	juice of 1 lemon
35g	sugar
25g	butter

Method

Peel and core the Bramley apples and chop to even sizes (this is to ensure they cook evenly). Place all the ingredients in a pan with a lid on a low heat and cook gently.

Stir occasionally and the apple will start to break down.

When almost cooked remove from the heat – the pan will keep cooking the apple – and allow to cool.

Use as it is or purée in a food processor for smooth apple sauce.

BROWN STOCK

For brown stocks, a few tomatoes and washed mushroom trimmings can also be added to improve the flavour. But take care as too many tomatoes can make the stock cloudy.

Ingredients

1 kg	beef bones
5 litres	cold water
500g	carrots, leek, celery, onion and garlic, cut into a fine dice
	sprig thyme, bay leaf and parsley stalks

Method

Brown the bones well on all sides. It is best to roast in a roasting tray as this will also release most of the fat.

Drain off any fat.

Deglaze with a little water and simmer for a few minutes.

Place the stock pot on to heat and brown the vegetables.

Add the thyme, parsley and bay leaf.

Add the browned bones and the liquid from the tray.

Simmer for approximately 8-12 hours.

Skim, strain and then reduce by half.

Cool quickly and refrigerate.

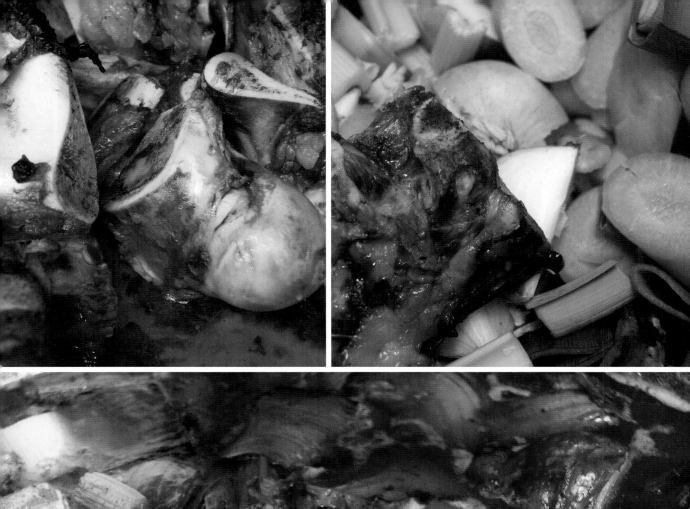

Fish Stock

Fish stock is only cooked for 20 minutes – any longer and the toxins in the bones will make the fish stock bitter.

Ingredients

1kg	white fish bones
250g	mix of white vegetables – onion, leek, celery, fennel and ½ clove garlic
½	lemon, juiced
	sprig parsley, thyme and bay
2 litres	cold water

Method

Heat a little oil in a large pan. Add the vegetables and sweat until soft – but without colour.

Wash the fish bones and add to the vegetables

Cover and sweat gently for 5 minutes.

Add the cold water and bring to the boil.

Skim off any scum and reduce to a gentle simmer.

Simmer for only 20 minutes, remove from the heat and strain. Put back on heat and reduce by half.

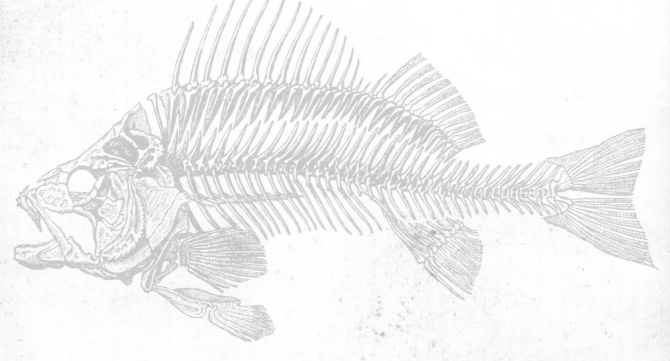

GROWN-UP TOMATO KETCHUP

(Makes about 500ml)

Every chef will secretly love tomato ketchup. It's a great everyday cupboard essential and you may have never even thought about making your own. But in the summer when we're awash in tomatoes there is something very satisfying about offering your guests real grown-up ketchup. This is one we developed at the Butchers Arms and it all came about when we ran out of Heinz. As is so often the case, necessity was the mother of invention. And we've never looked back. Our own Grown-Up Tomato Ketchup is the one we serve.

Ingredients

	drizzle extra virgin olive oil
2	large red onions, peeled and chopped
2	sticks celery, trimmed and chopped
1	bulb fennel, trimmed and chopped
2	cloves garlic, peeled and smashed
½	fresh red chilli, seeds removed and finely chopped
4cm	ginger peeled and roughly chopped
	small bunch basil leaves, picked and stalks chopped
2	cloves
1tsp	ground black pepper
	pinch Cornish sea salt
½ tsp	coriander seeds
2	bay leaves
1	blade mace
250ml	red wine vinegar
100g	demerara sugar
2.250kg	fresh ripe plum tomatoes, deseeded
2kg	tinned plum tomatoes, chopped
500g	tomato purée

Method

Heat a large heavy-bottom pan and add the olive oil. Add the red onion, celery, fennel, garlic, red chilli, basil stalks and ginger.

Cook over a gentle heat without colour for 10-15 minutes stirring occasionally.

Add the cloves, ground black pepper, salt, coriander seeds, bay and mace, and cook for a further 2 minutes.

Add all the tomatoes and purée.

Bring to the boil and then simmer until the sauce reduces by half.

Add the basil leaves and whiz the sauce in a food processor until smooth.

Pass through a fine sieve twice to make it really smooth. Put the sauce into a clean pan with the vinegar and sugar.

Return to the heat and simmer until the mixture has a thick ketchup consistency.

Correct the seasoning.

The grown-up tomato ketchup is now ready to be put into sterilised bottles sealed tight and placed in a cool dark place or the fridge. This should keep for 6 months and is great with steak and chips.

Tip: Try using green or yellow tomatoes.

Yorkshire Piccalilli

Ingredients

3kg	cauliflower cut into small florets
1kg	onion diced
3	cucumber deseeded and diced
480g	salt
1 tbsp	turmeric
1 tbsp	mustard
1 tbsp	ground ginger
240g	sugar
1.65 litres	vinegar
60g	cornflour

Method

Salt the cauliflower and leave for 24 hours.

Wash the cauliflower in cold water to remove the salt.

Place all ingredients except the cucumber in a pan and boil, skim and simmer until thick and liquid has reduced.

Add the diced cucumber and mix in and leave to cool.

This can be placed into jars and kept in the fridge.

HOLLANDAISE SAUCE

Another great sauce to serve with a juicy steak.

Ingredients

6	crushed peppercorns
1 tbsp	vinegar
2	egg yolks
200g	butter
	salt and cayenne pepper

Method

Place the peppercorns and vinegar in a small pan and reduce by one third.

Add 1 tablespoon of cold water and allow to cool.

Mix in the yolks with a whisk.

Return to a gentle heat, whisking continuously until thick – this is known as the sabayon stage. Remove from heat and allow to cool slightly.

Whisk in the melted butter slowly until thoroughly combined. Correct the seasoning and pass through a fine chinois.

Serve.

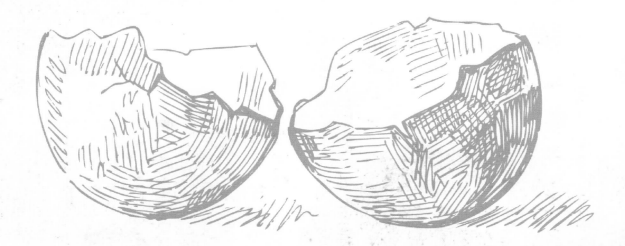

SOUBISE SAUCE

Ingredients

25g	butter
400g	onions, sliced thin
125ml	white wine
250g	cream
	marjoram stalks
	thyme stalks

Method

Sweat the onions in the butter without colour. Add the thyme and marjoram stalks.

Add the white wine and reduce by half, then add the cream and bring to the boil.

Reduce until the sauce has thickened slightly.

Season with salt and pepper, then whisk until smooth with a hand blender.

Pass through a fine sieve.

MAYONNAISE

(Makes about 275ml)

Ingredients

2	egg yolks
1 tsp	white wine vinegar
½ tsp	Dijon mustard
	pinch salt
	pinch pepper
250ml	olive oil
2 tsp	hot water (approximately)

Method

Place the egg yolks, vinegar, mustard, salt and pepper in a bowl and mix thoroughly with a whisk. Slowly add the olive oil, whisk continuously a drop at a time at first until the oil is emulsified in the egg yolks. If the mayonnaise becomes too thick then add a little hot water.

Use the oil at lukewarm temperature (approximately 20°C).

The hot water will also stabilise the mayonnaise.

Store in the fridge with an airtight lid.

If the mayonnaise separates e.g. if the oil is added too quickly, then place a fresh egg yolk in a clean basin with a little splash of vinegar, whisk in a little oil to start thickening then whisk in the separated mayonnaise little by little.

TARTAR SAUCE

(Makes about 275ml)

Ingredients

25g	fine capers, chopped
50g	gherkins, chopped
1 tsp	chopped fine herbs or parsley
	lemon zest and juice

Method

Add to the mayonnaise recipe.

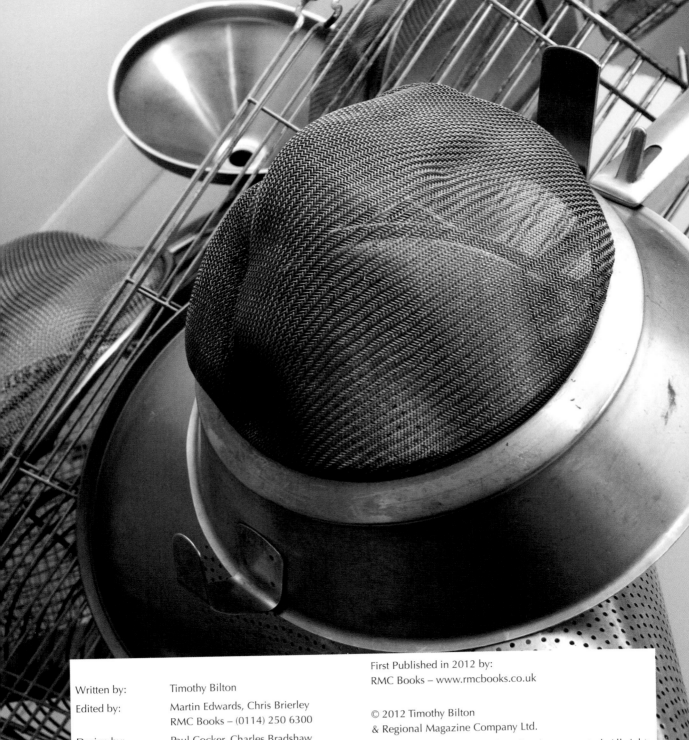

Written by: Timothy Bilton

Edited by: Martin Edwards, Chris Brierley
                   RMC Books – (0114) 250 6300

Design by: Paul Cocker, Charles Bradshaw
                   RMC Books – (0114) 250 6300

Photography by: David Walker –
                   www.davidwalkerphotography.co.uk

Contributors: Adele Bilton, Susan Pape, Katy Ford

First Published in 2012 by:
RMC Books – www.rmcbooks.co.uk